Amazing

BATS

Coloring Book For Adults

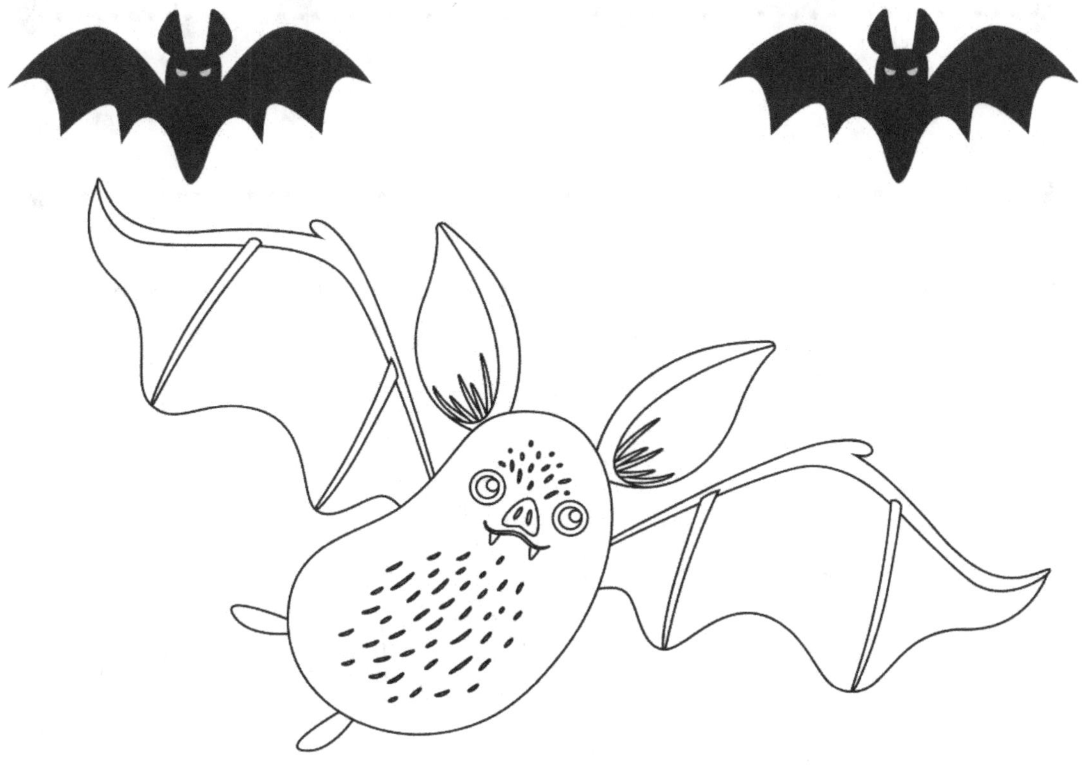

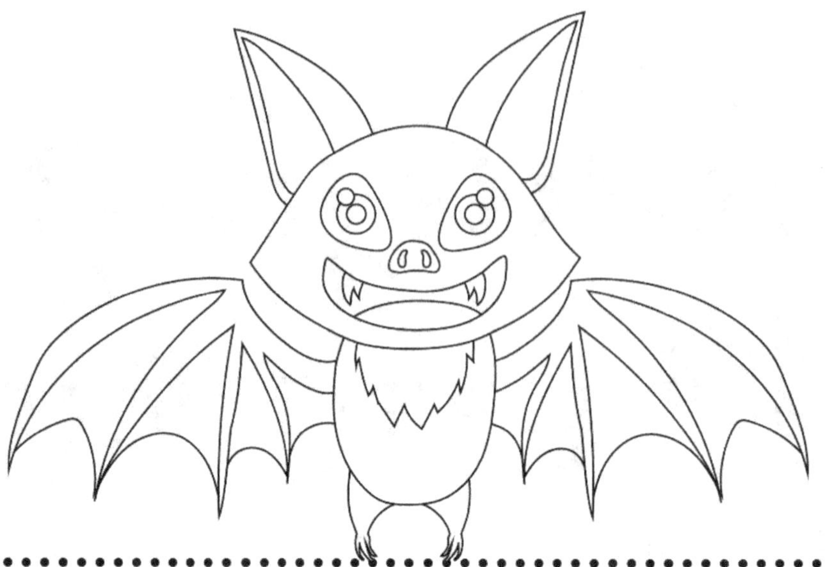

This Book Belongs To

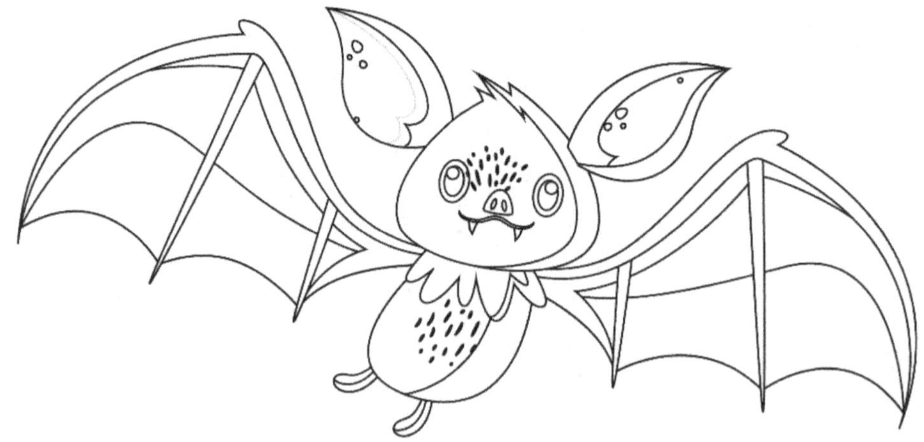

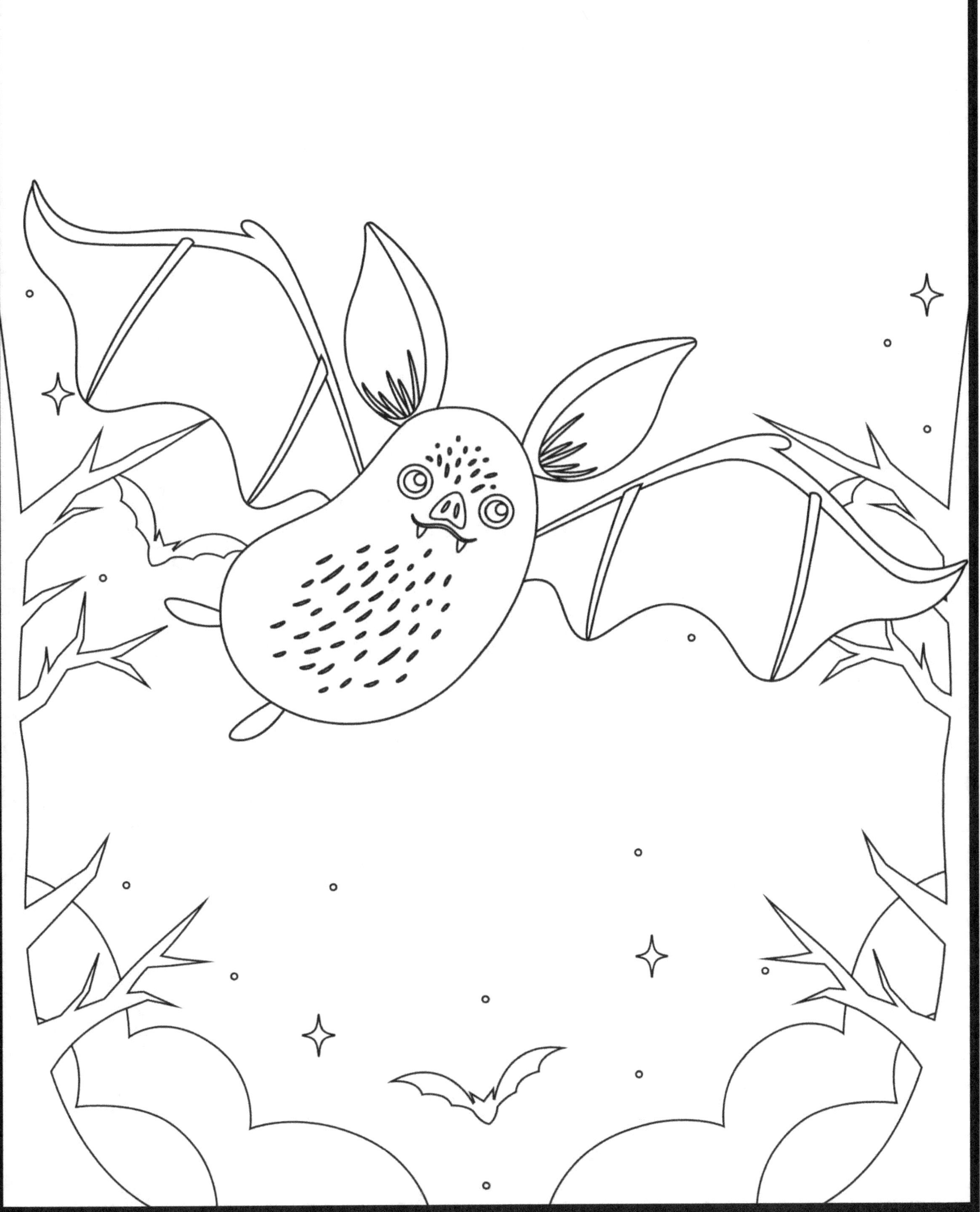

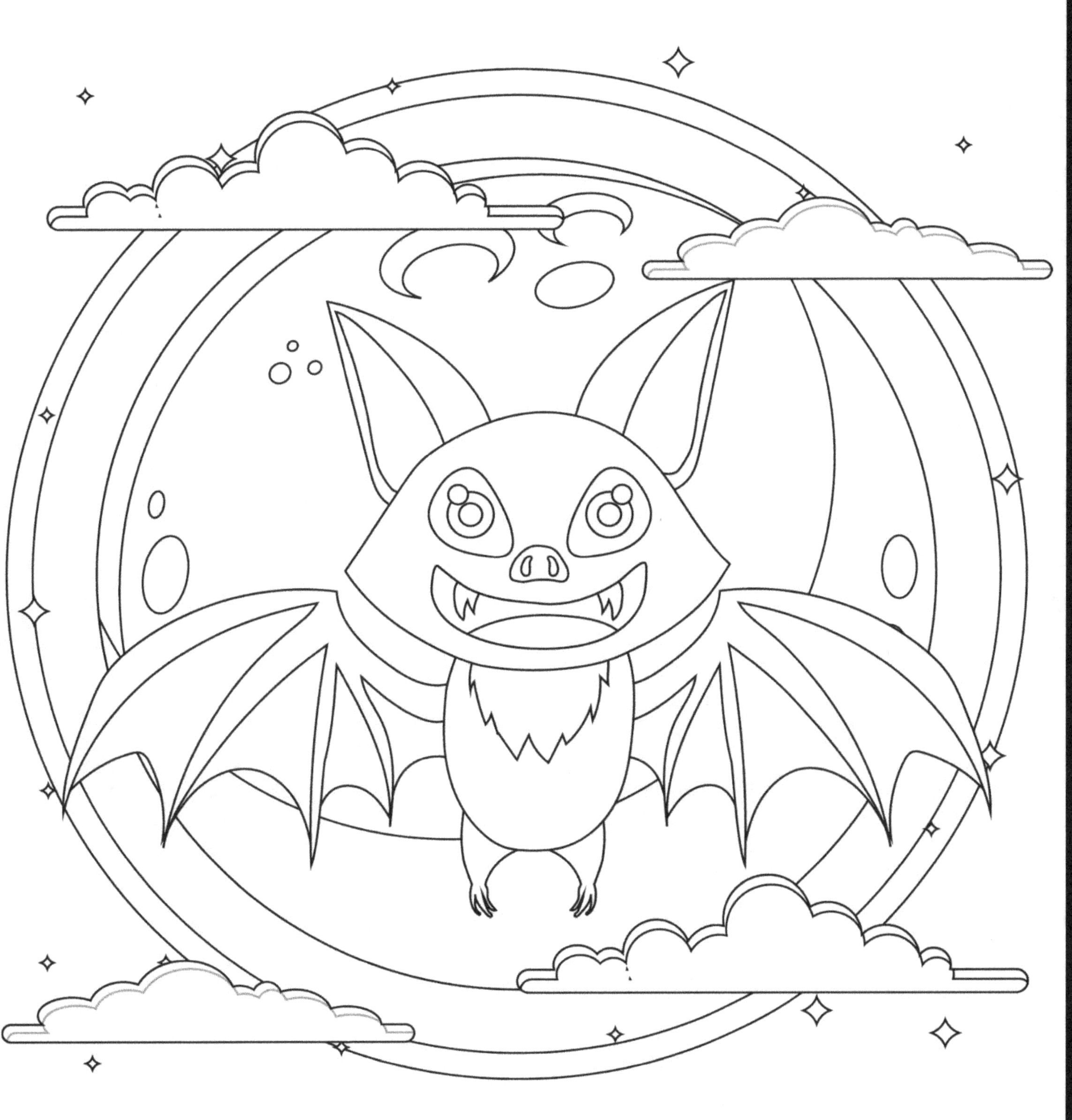

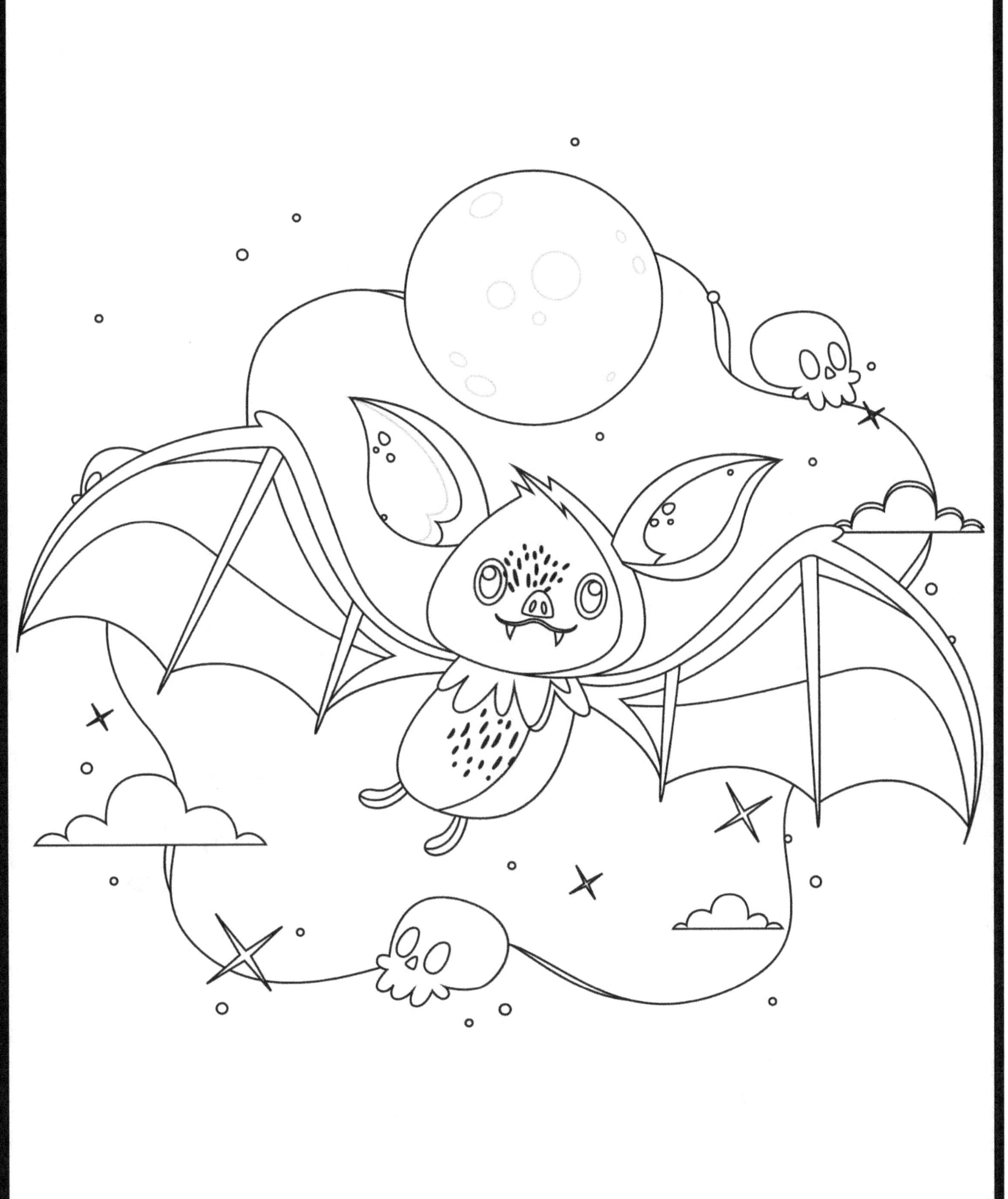

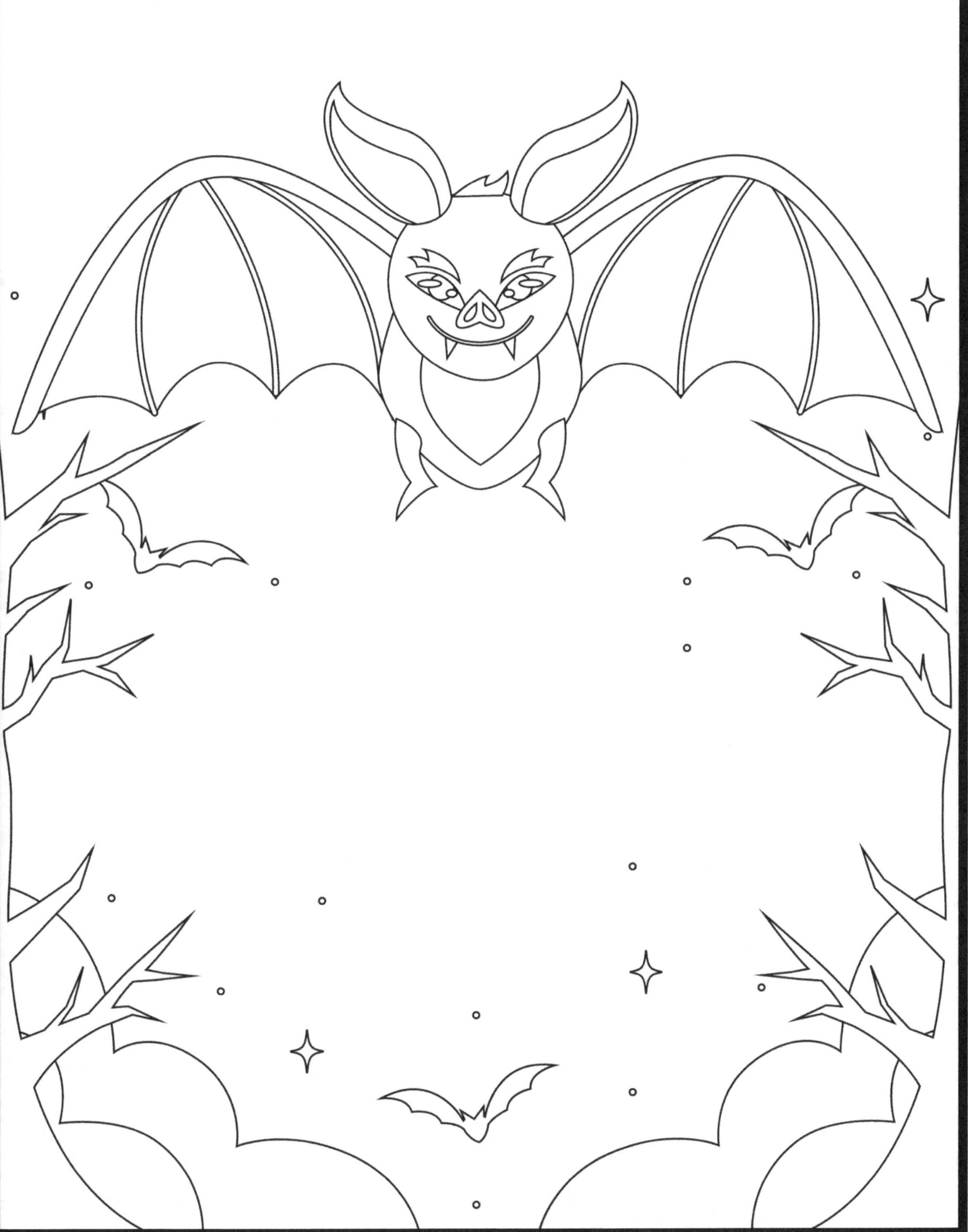

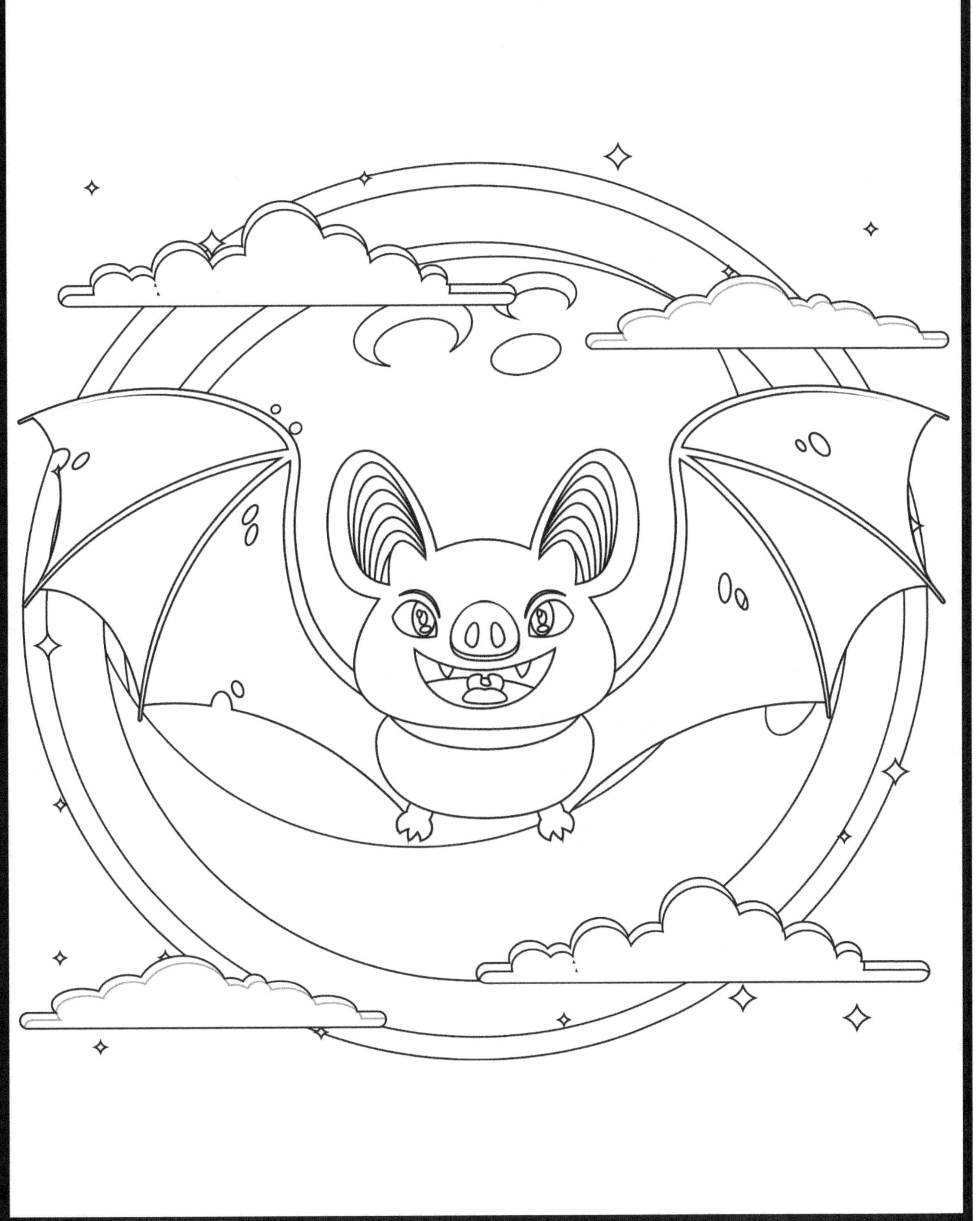

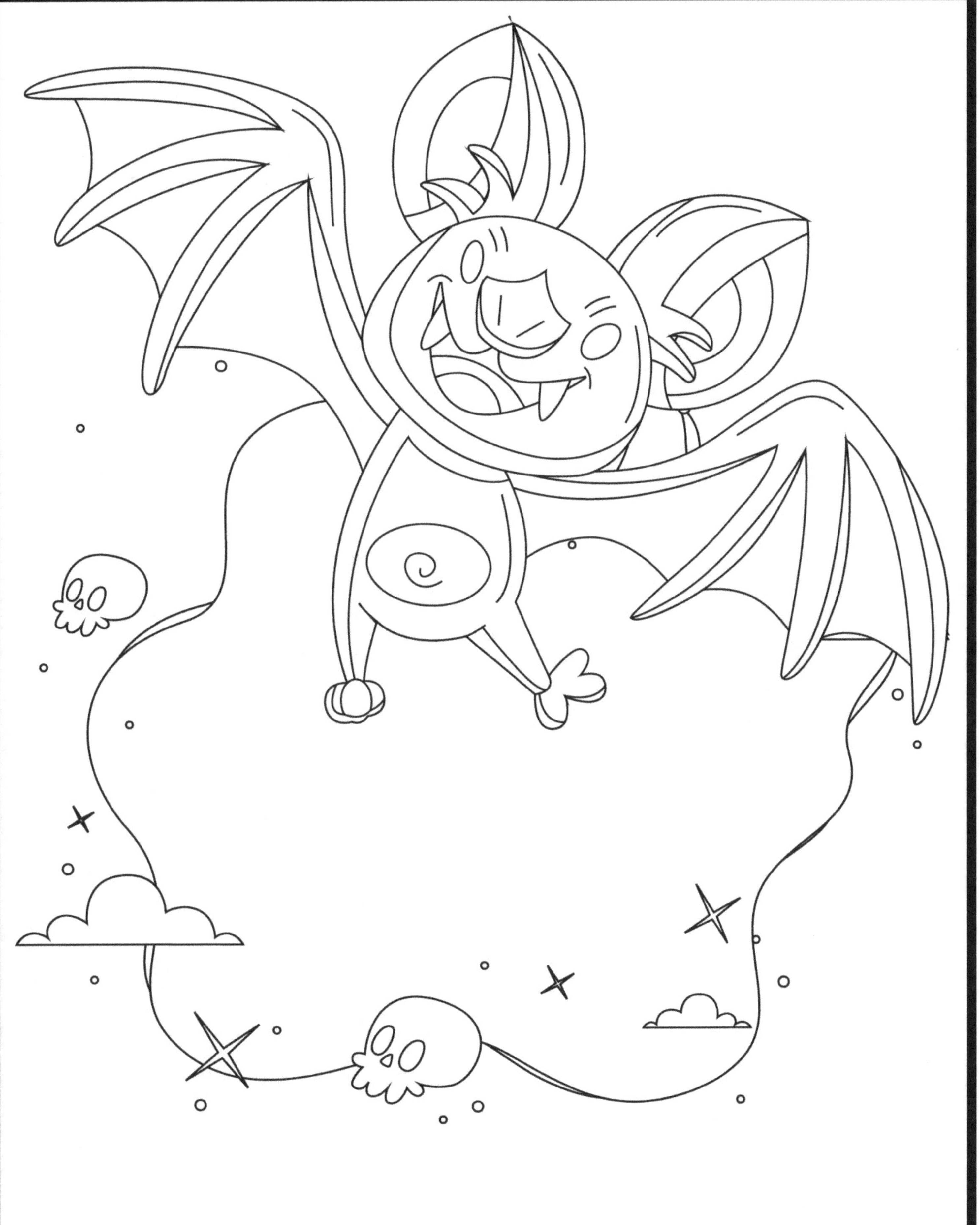

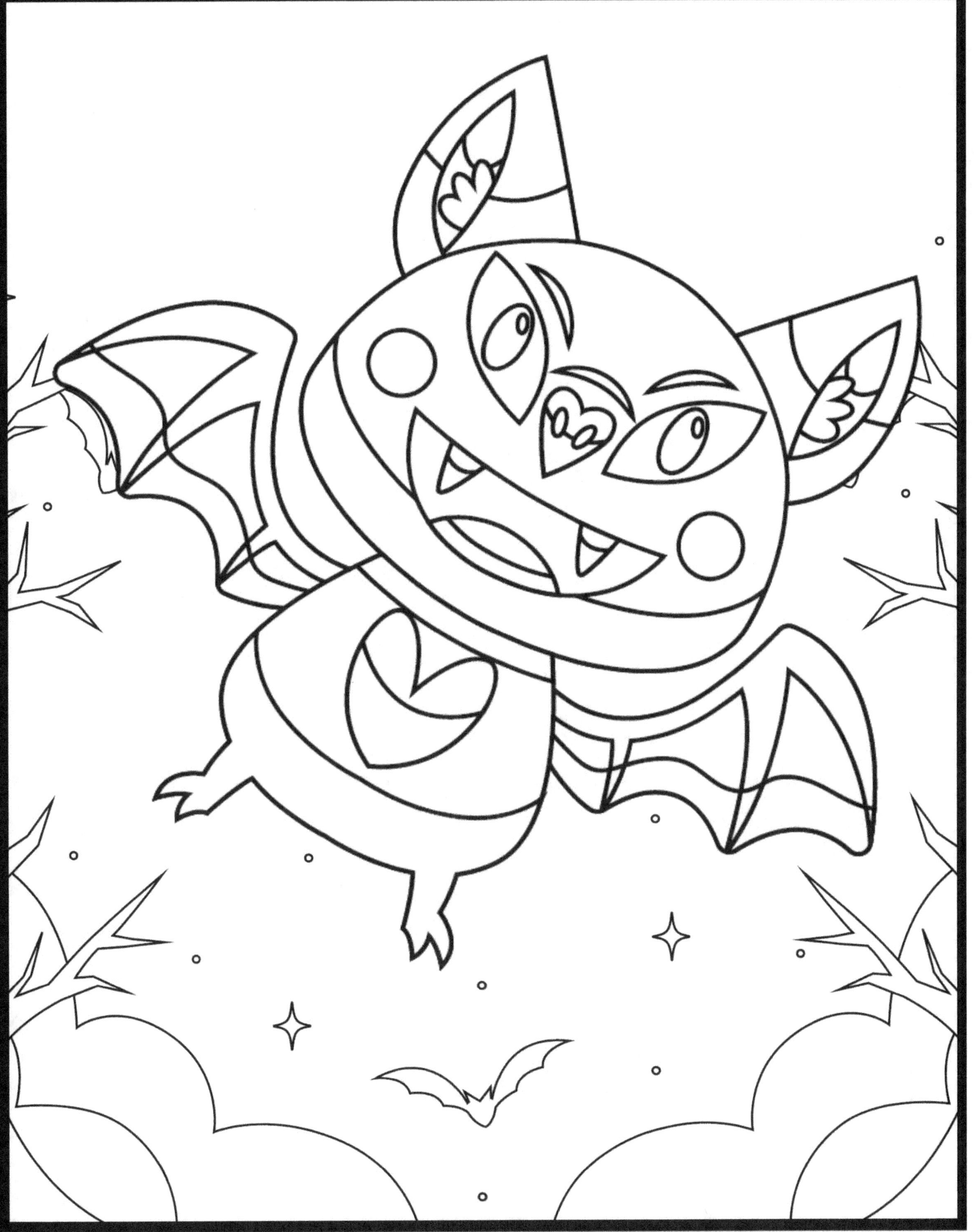

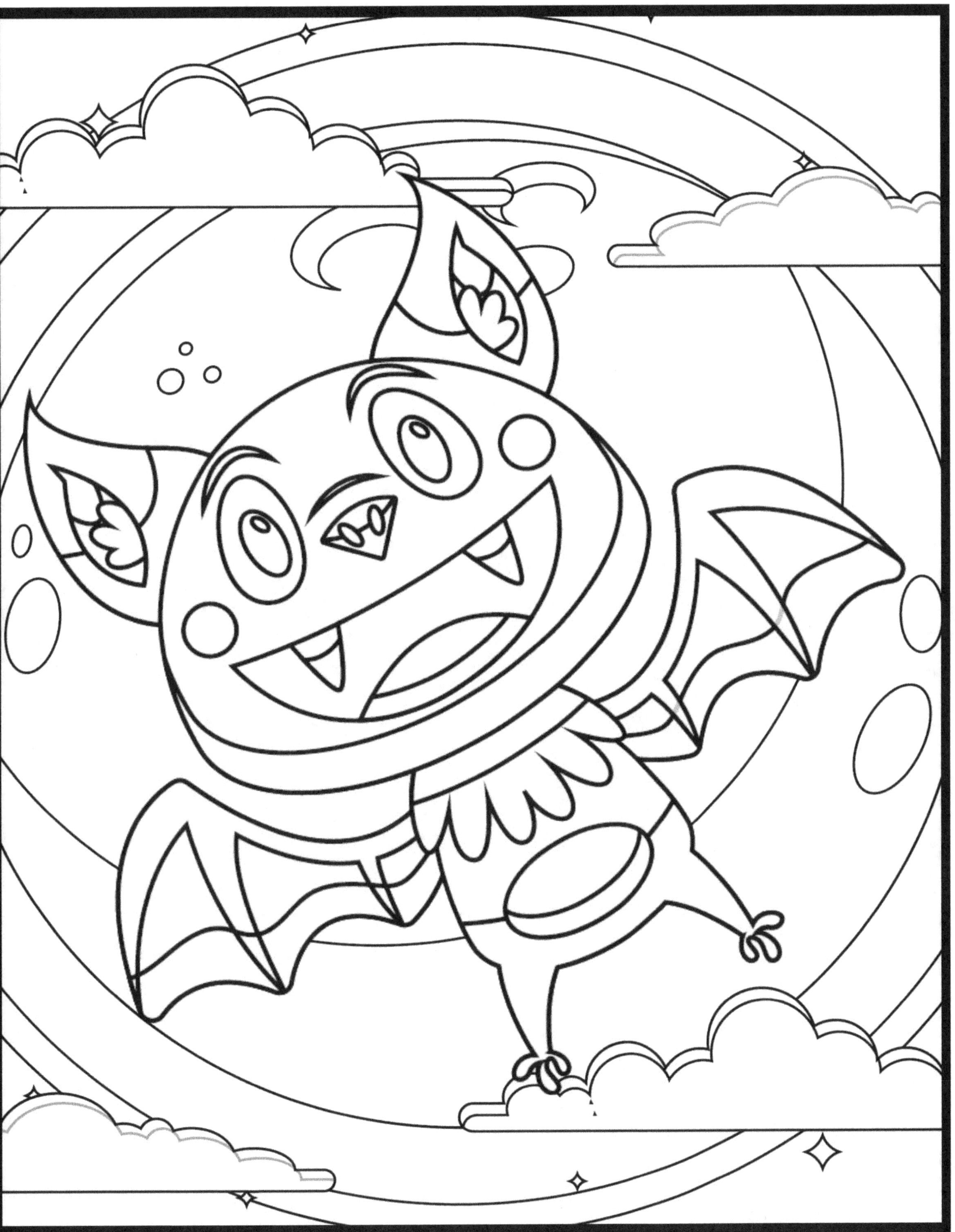

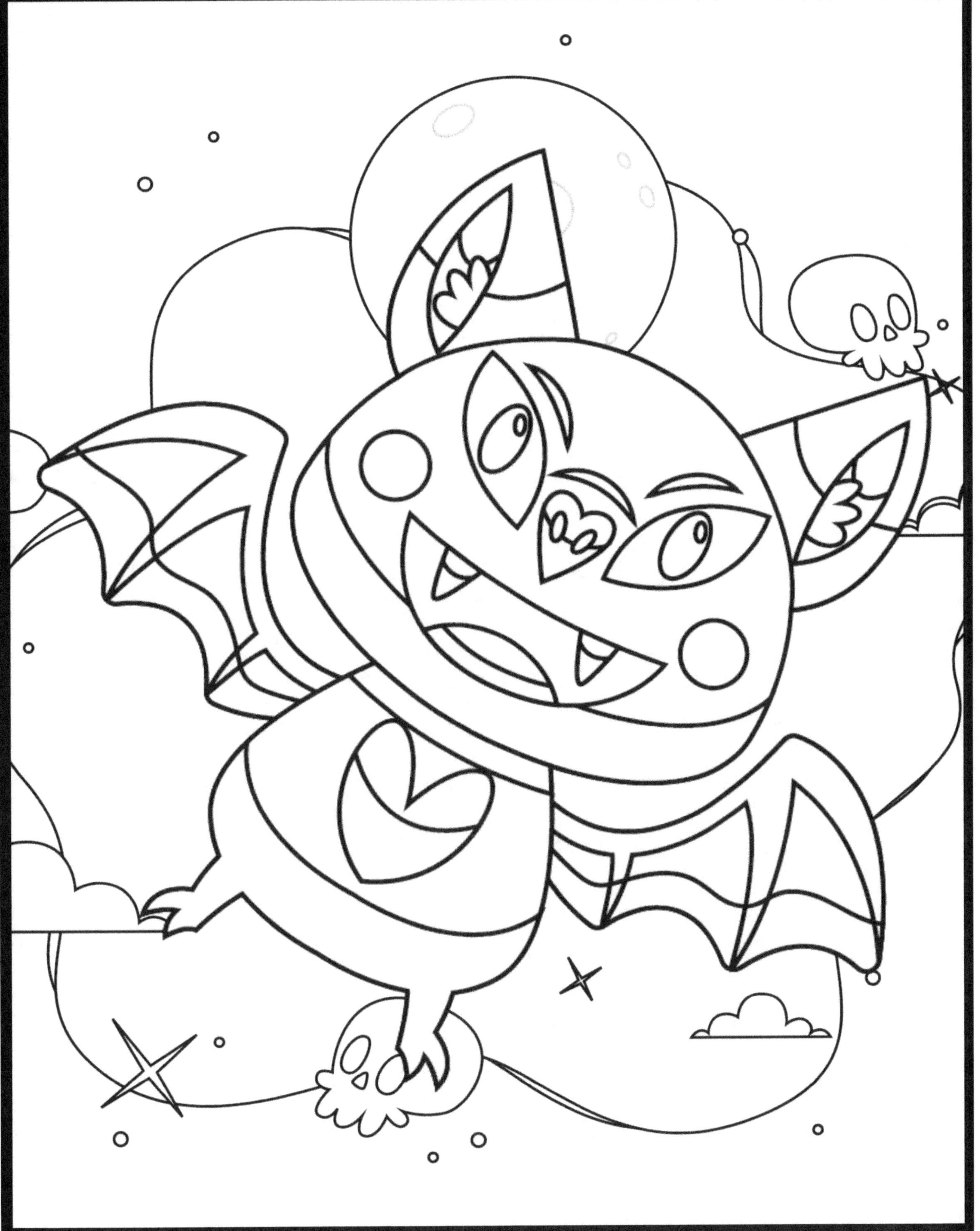

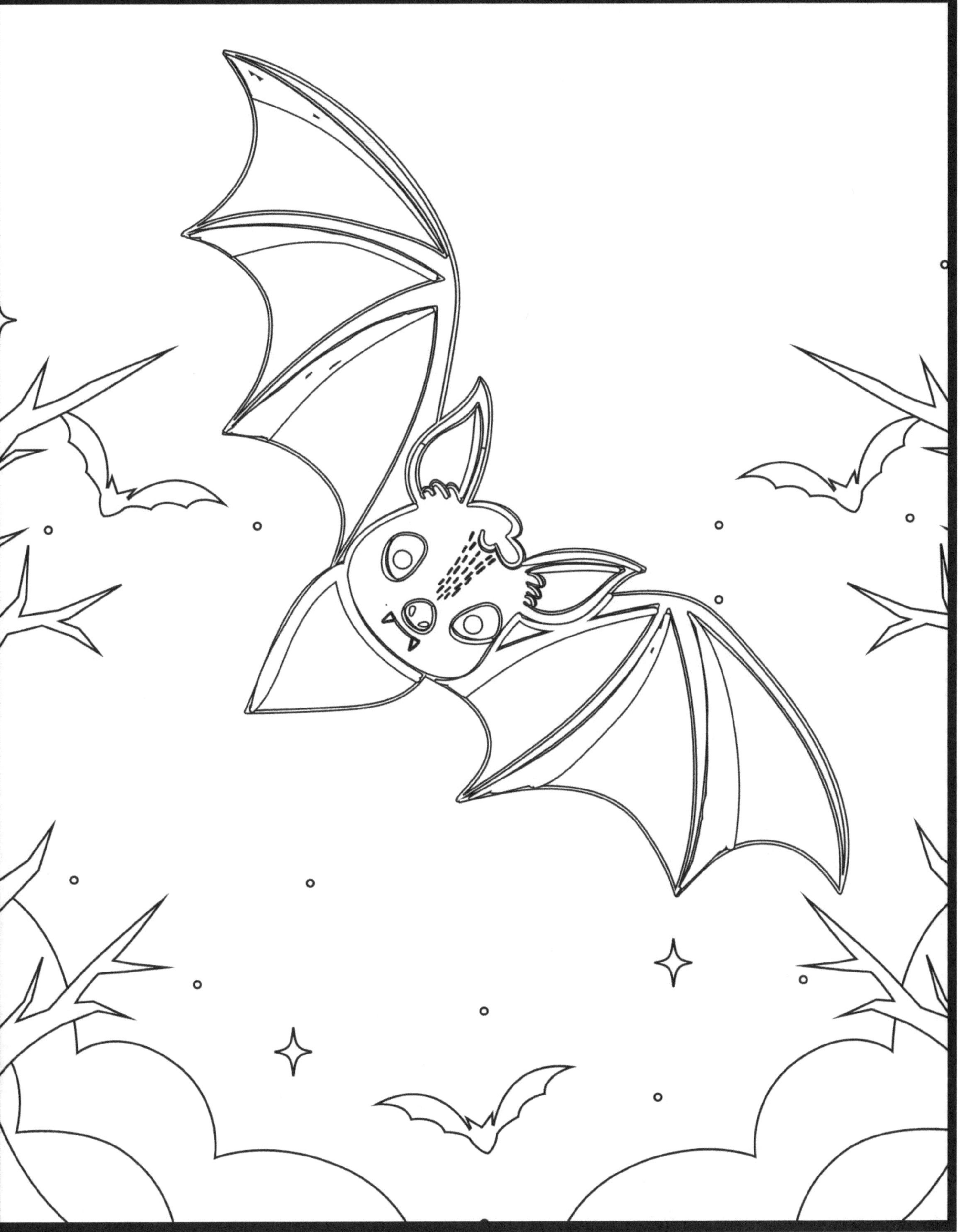

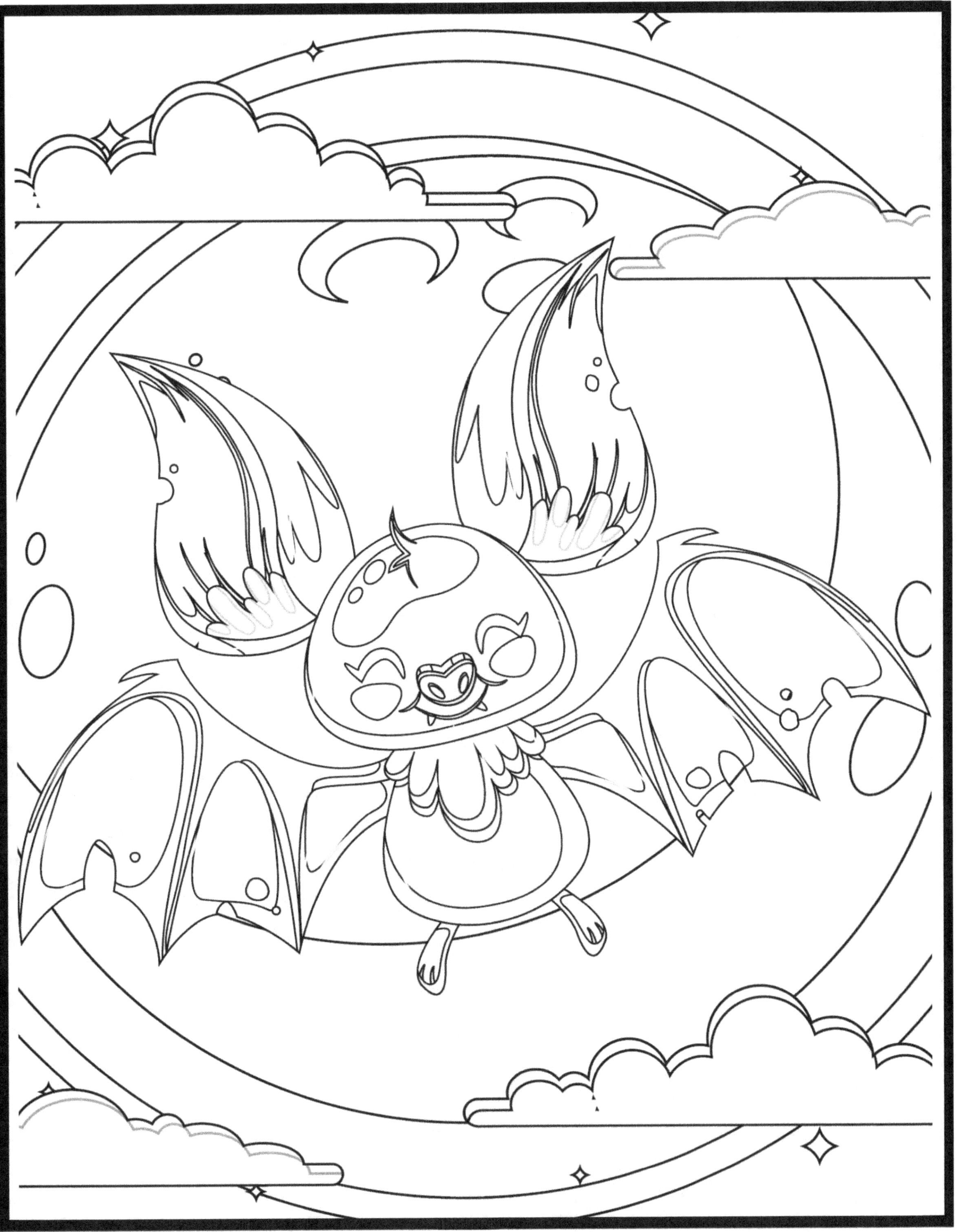

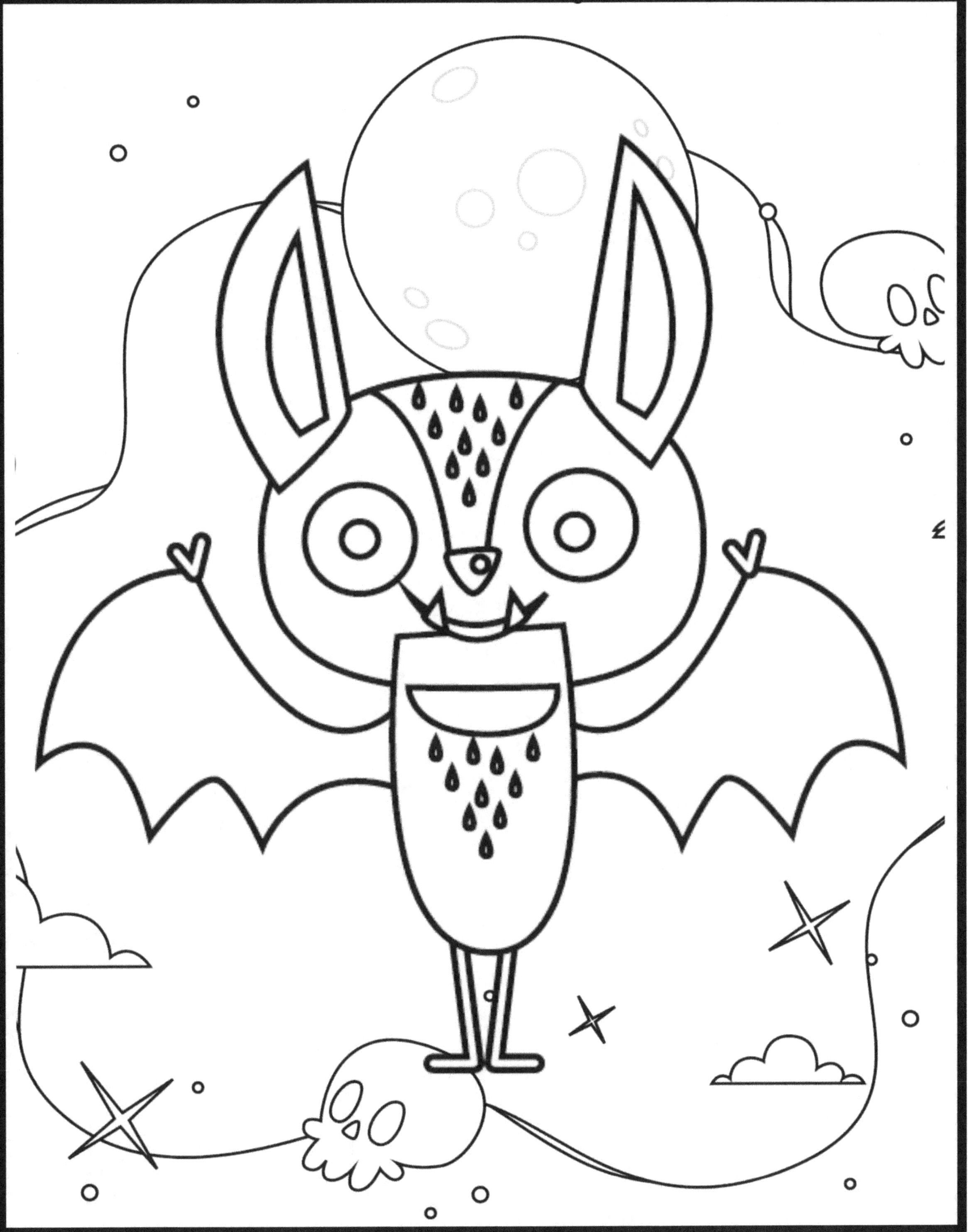

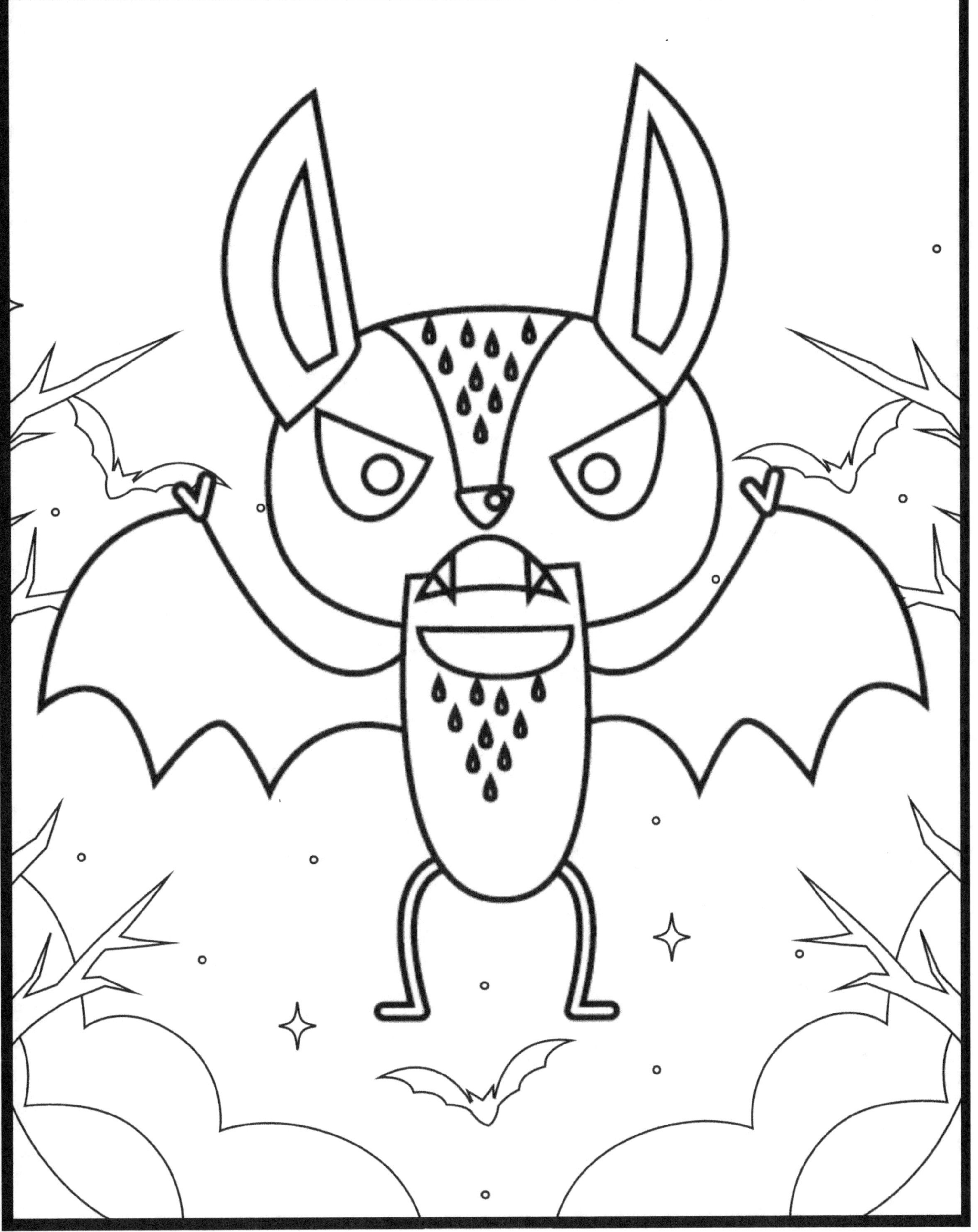

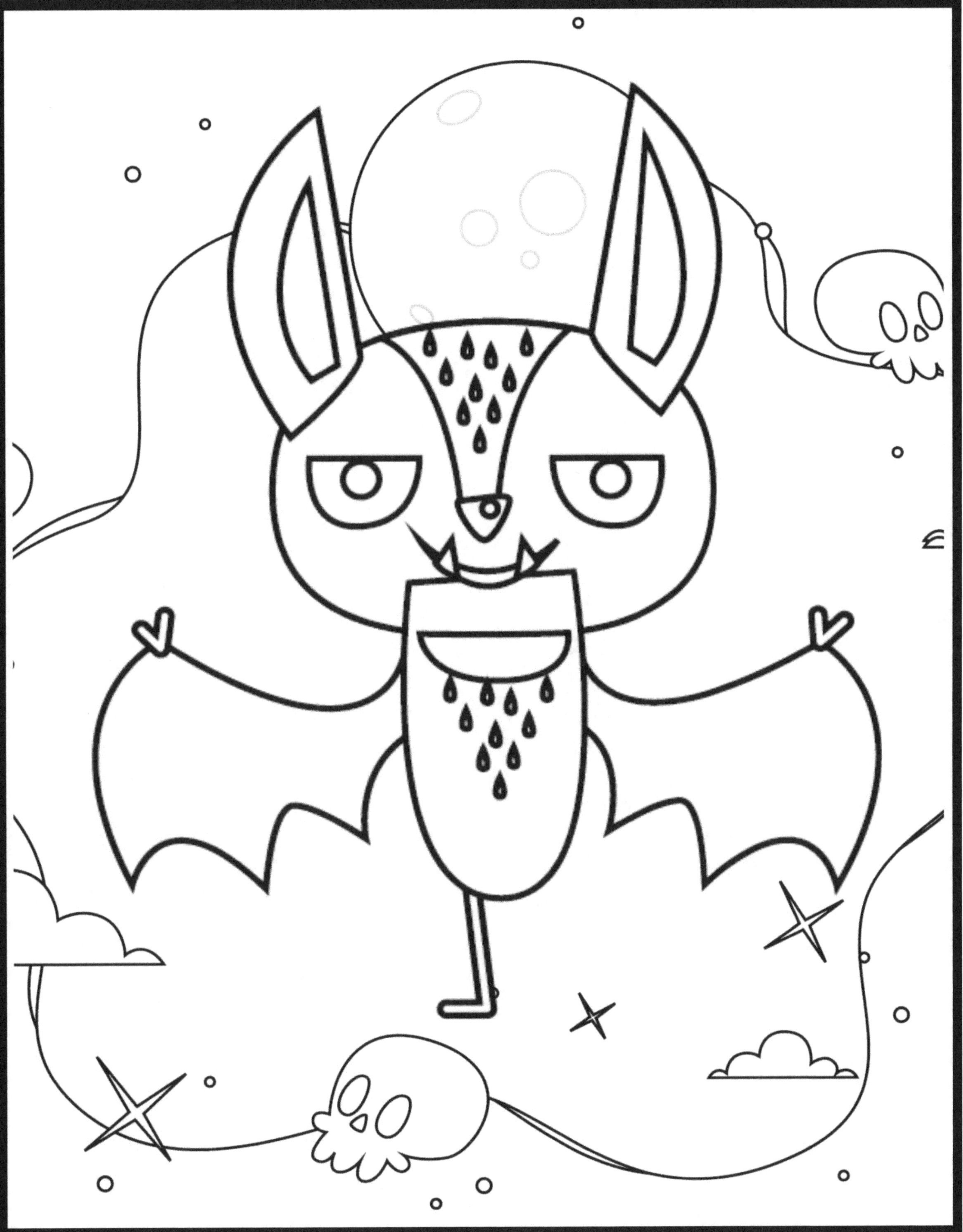

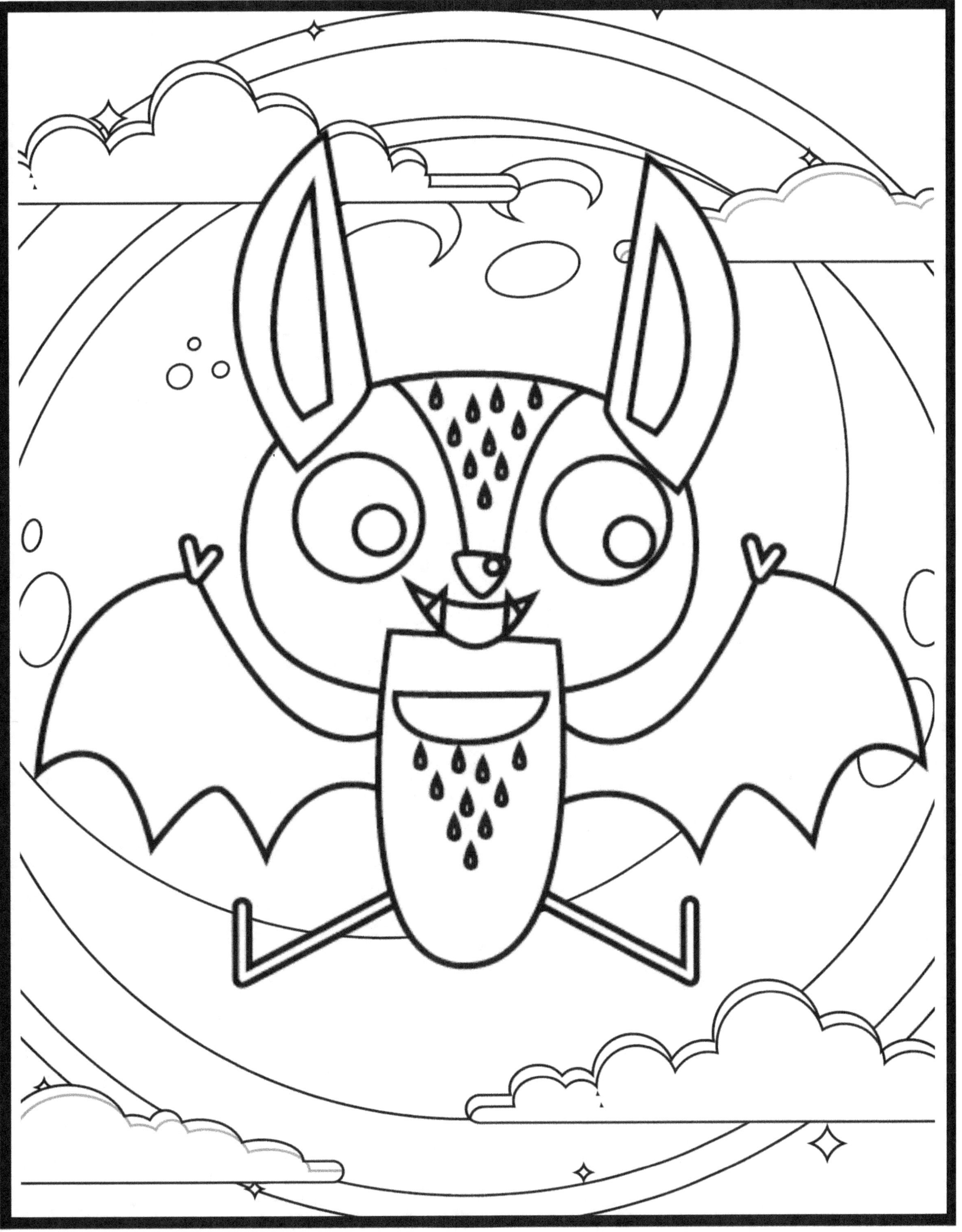

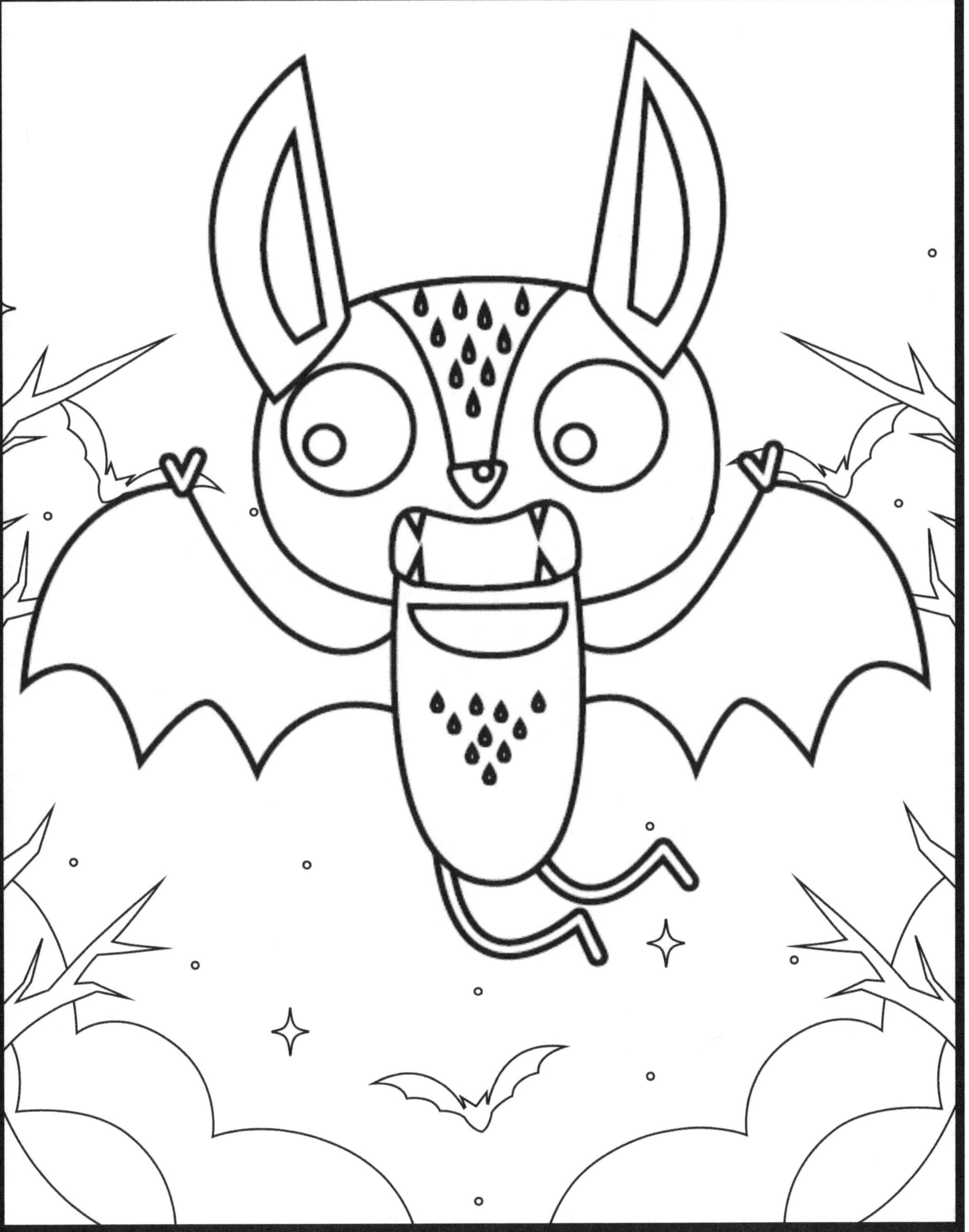

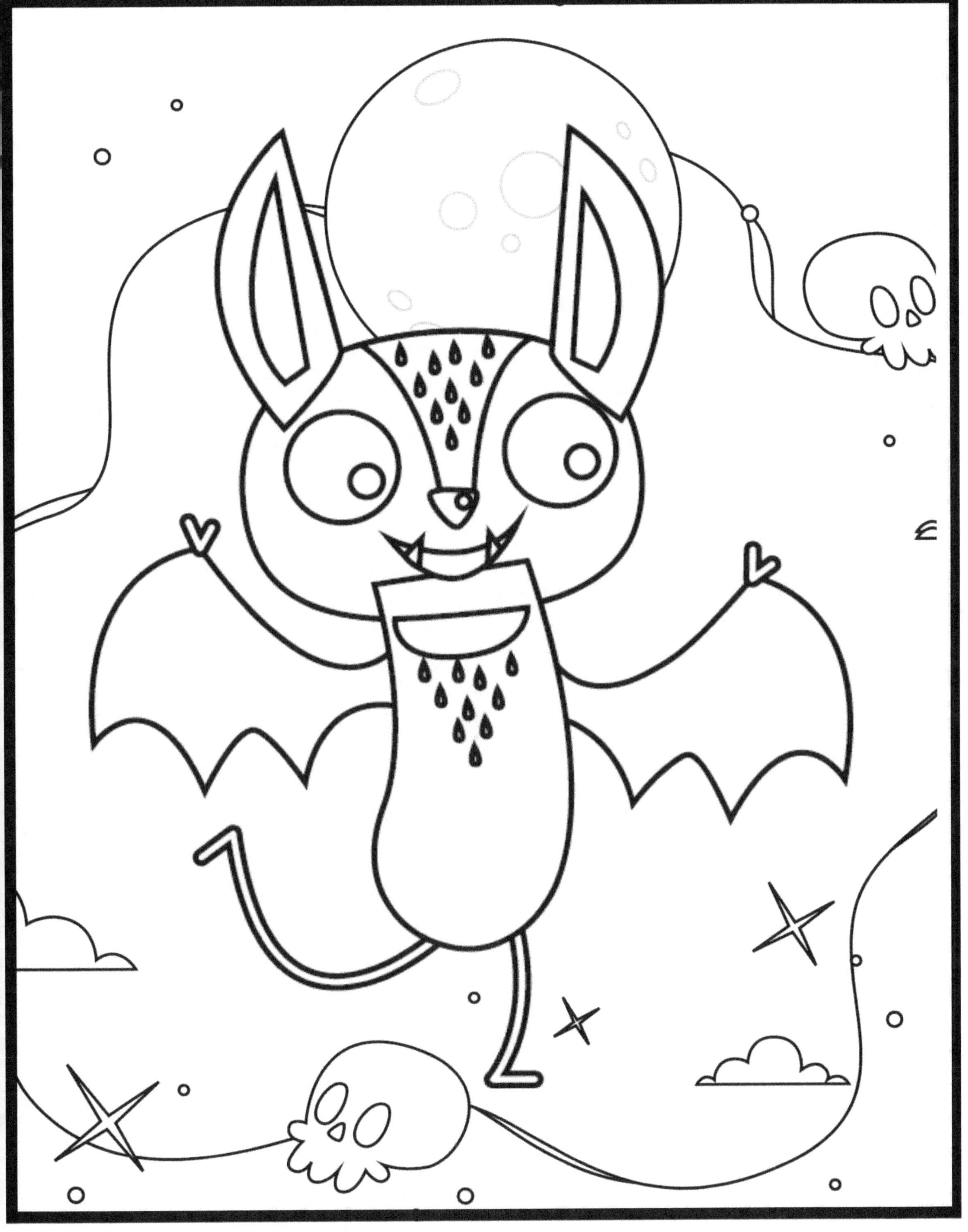

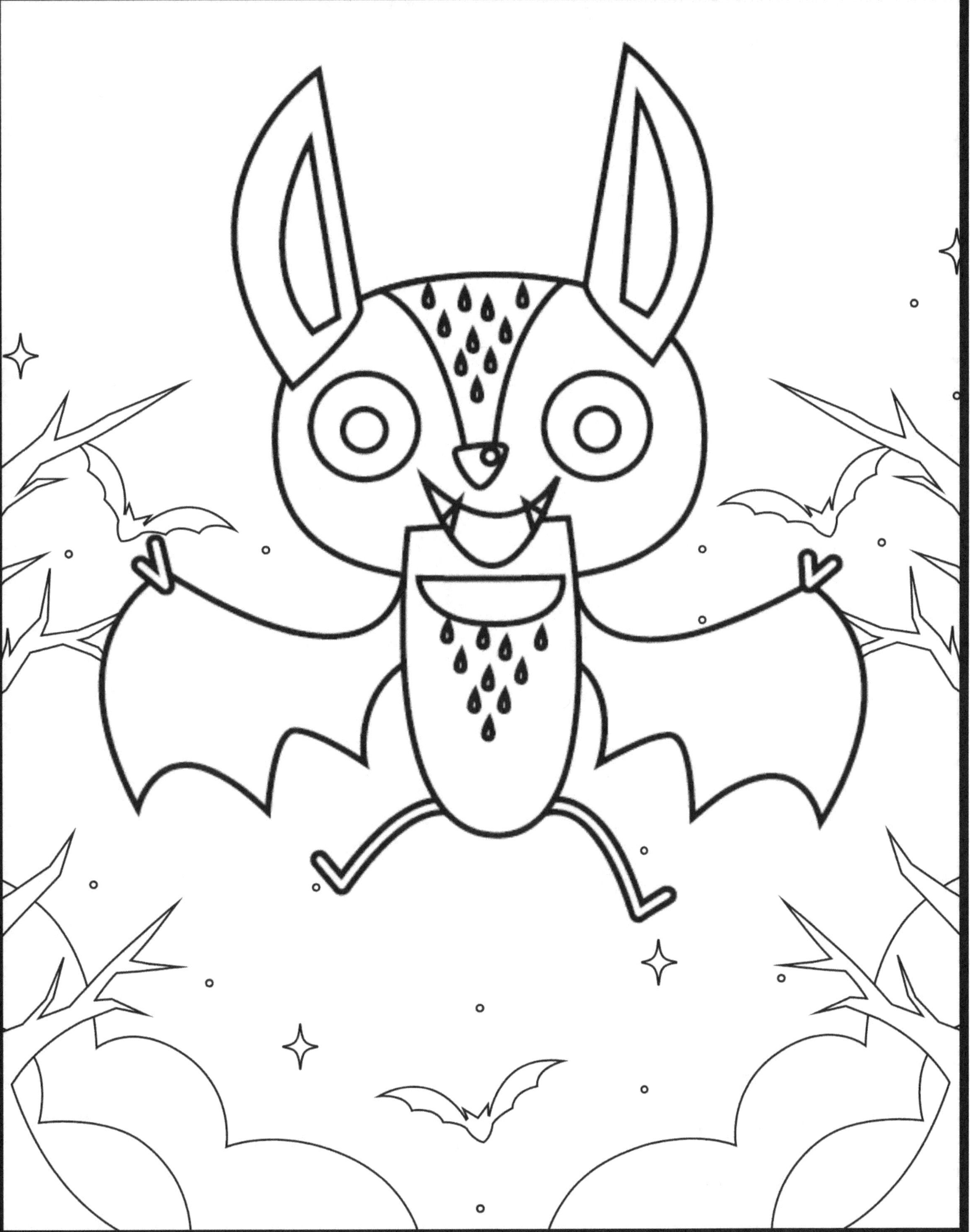

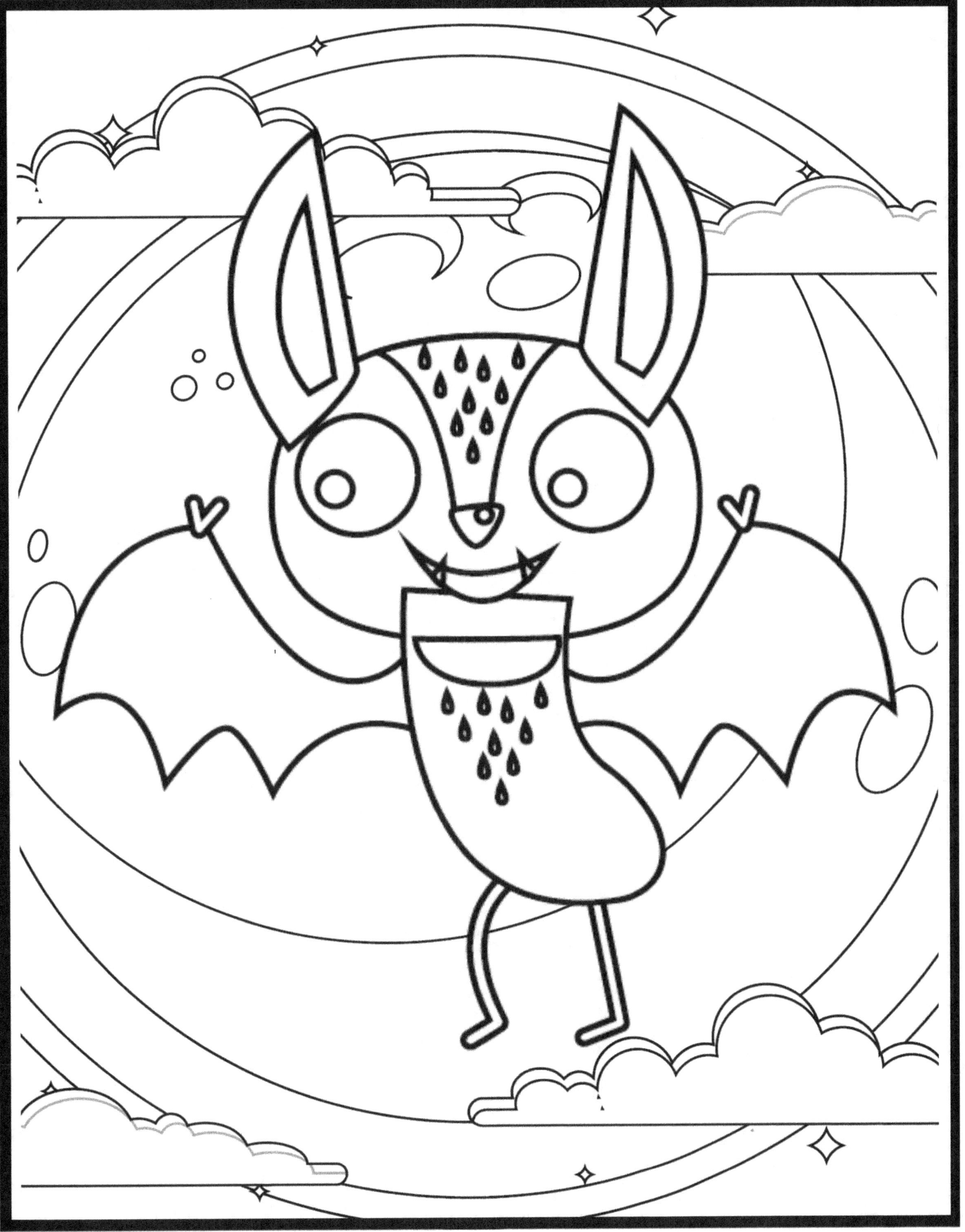

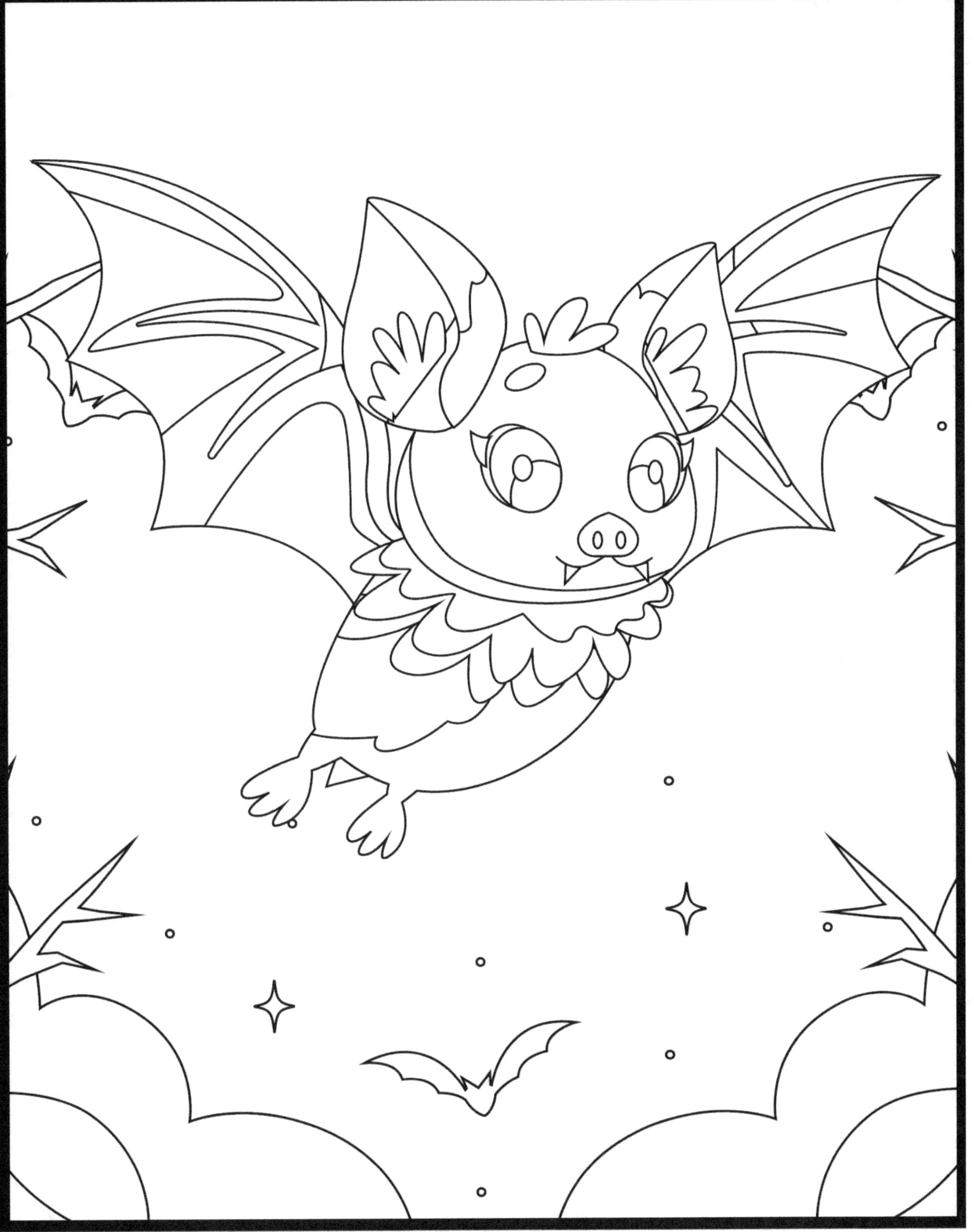

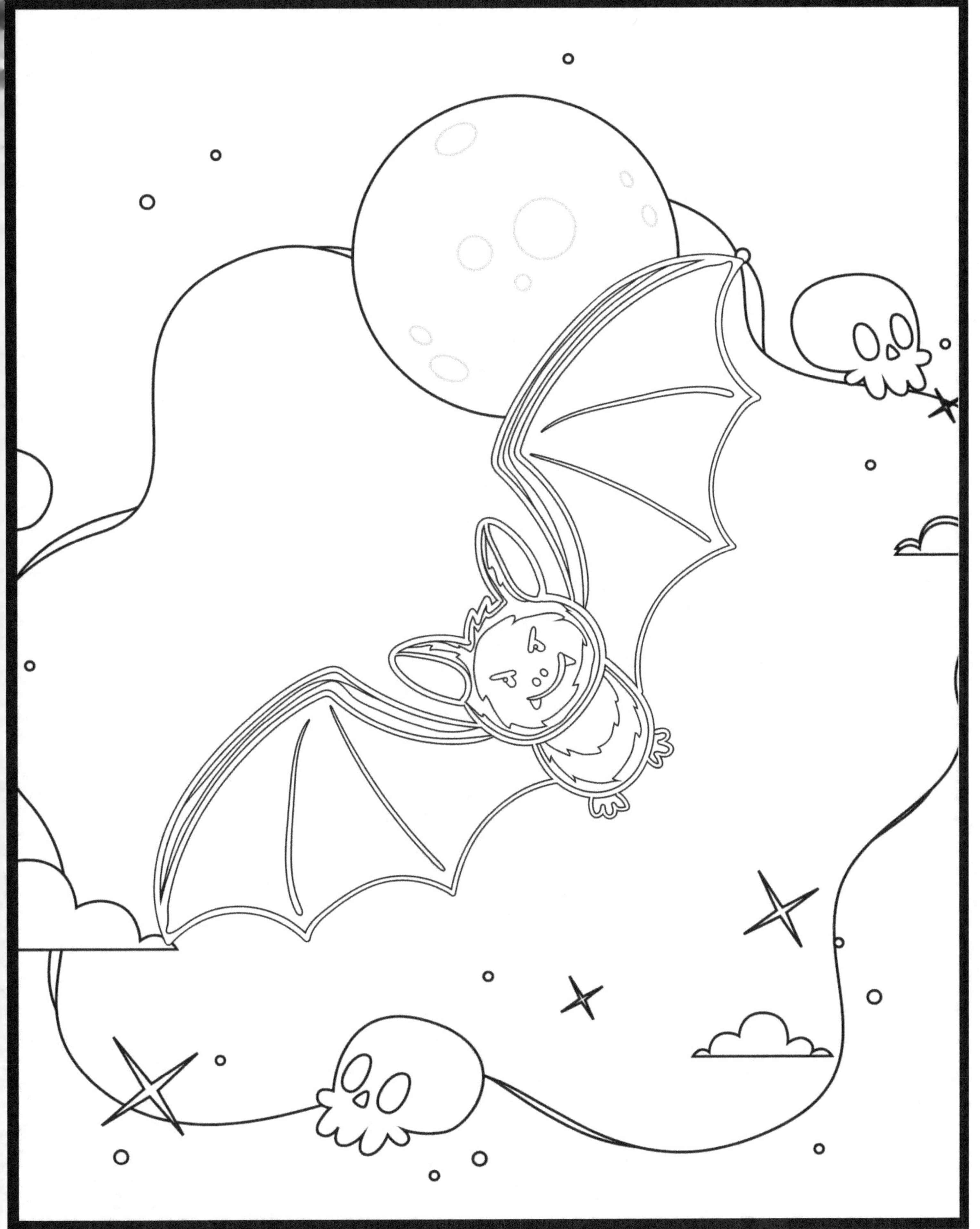

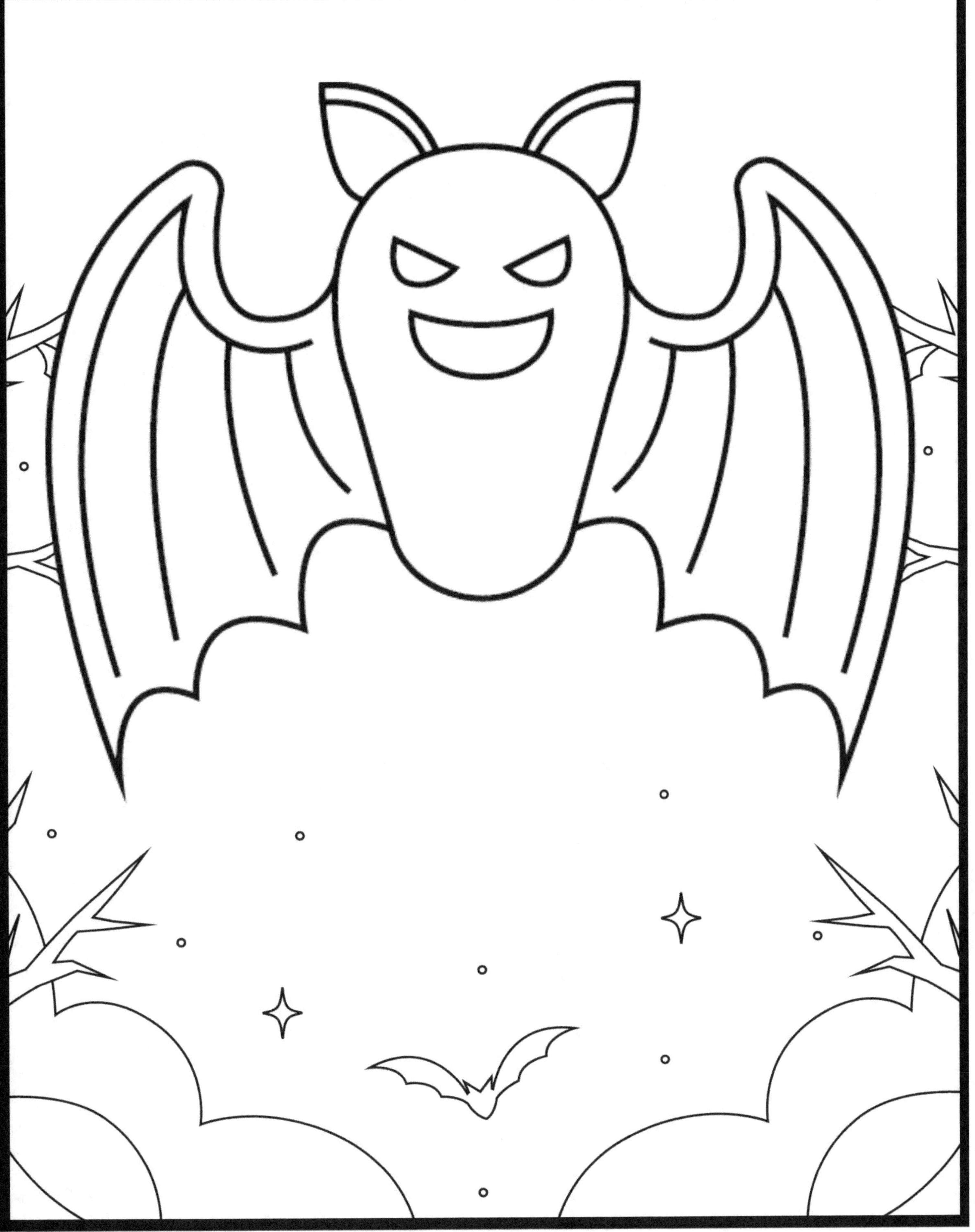

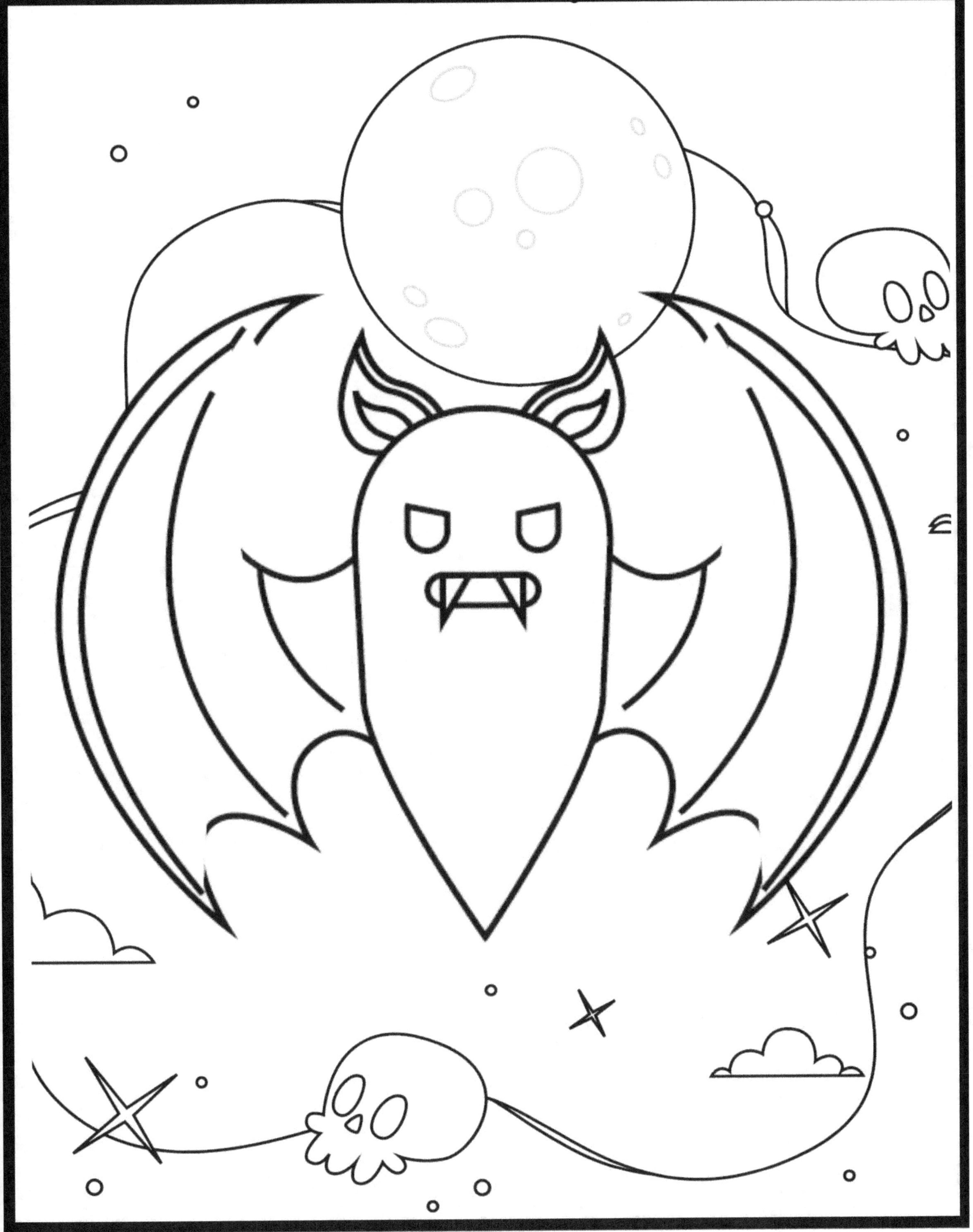

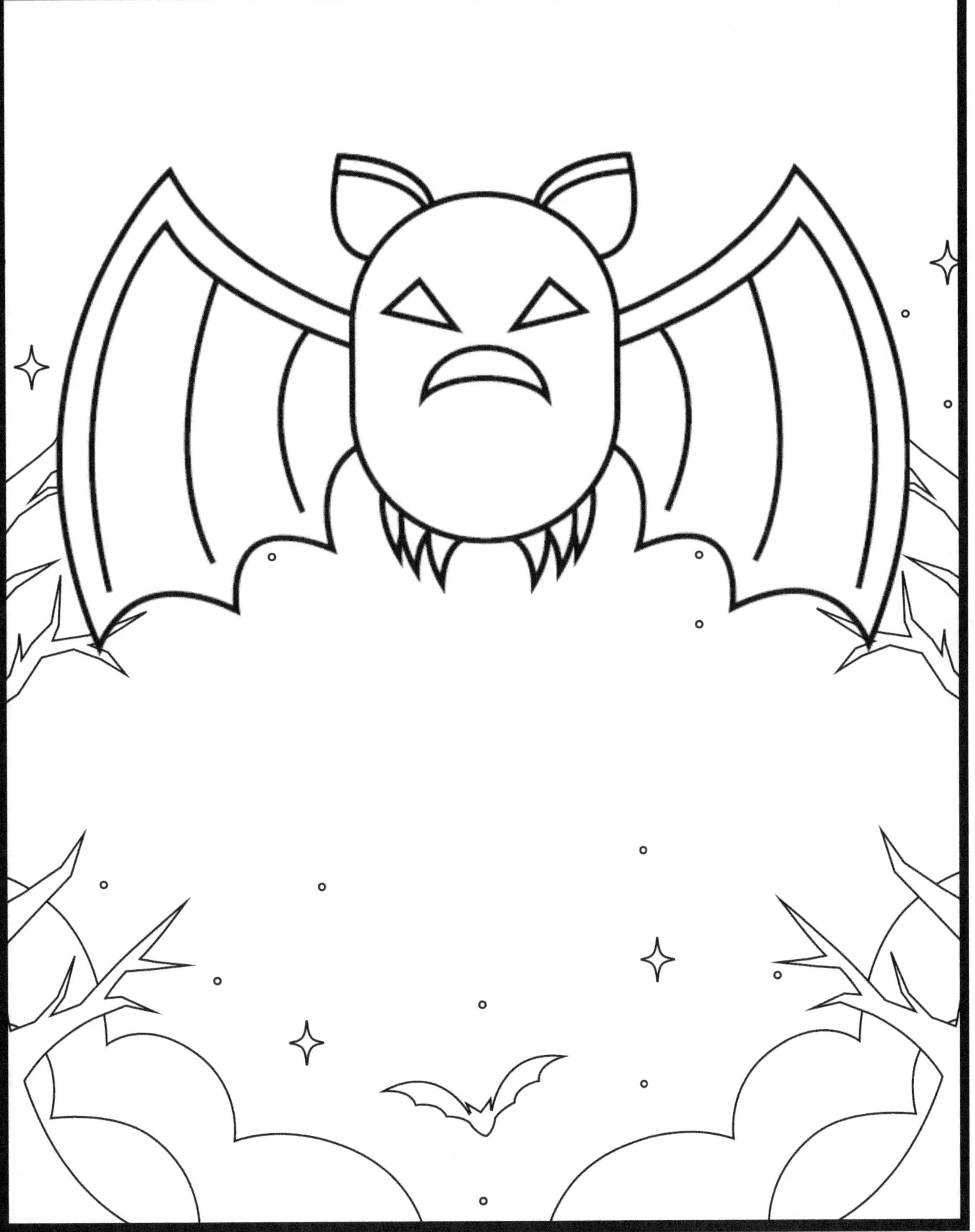

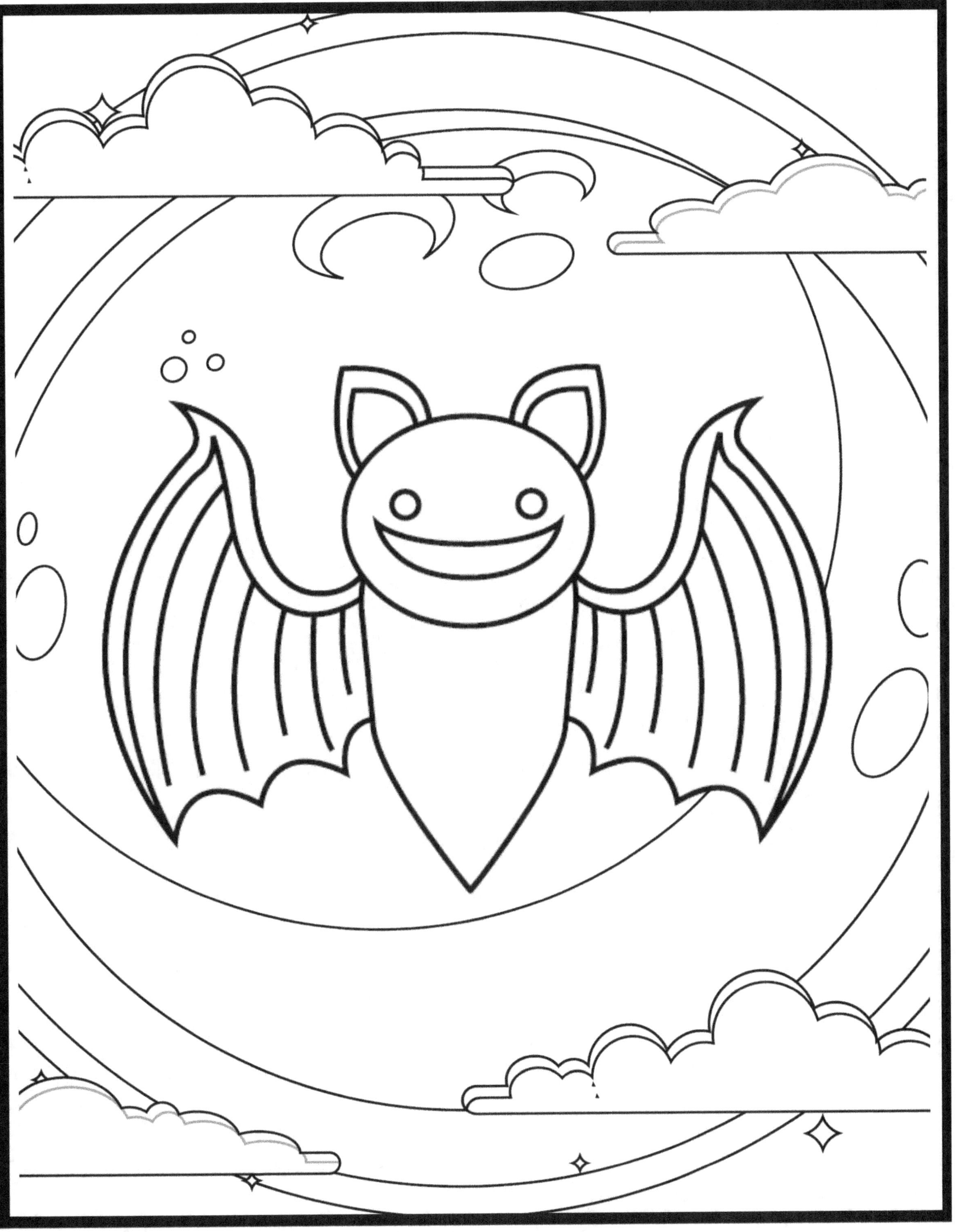

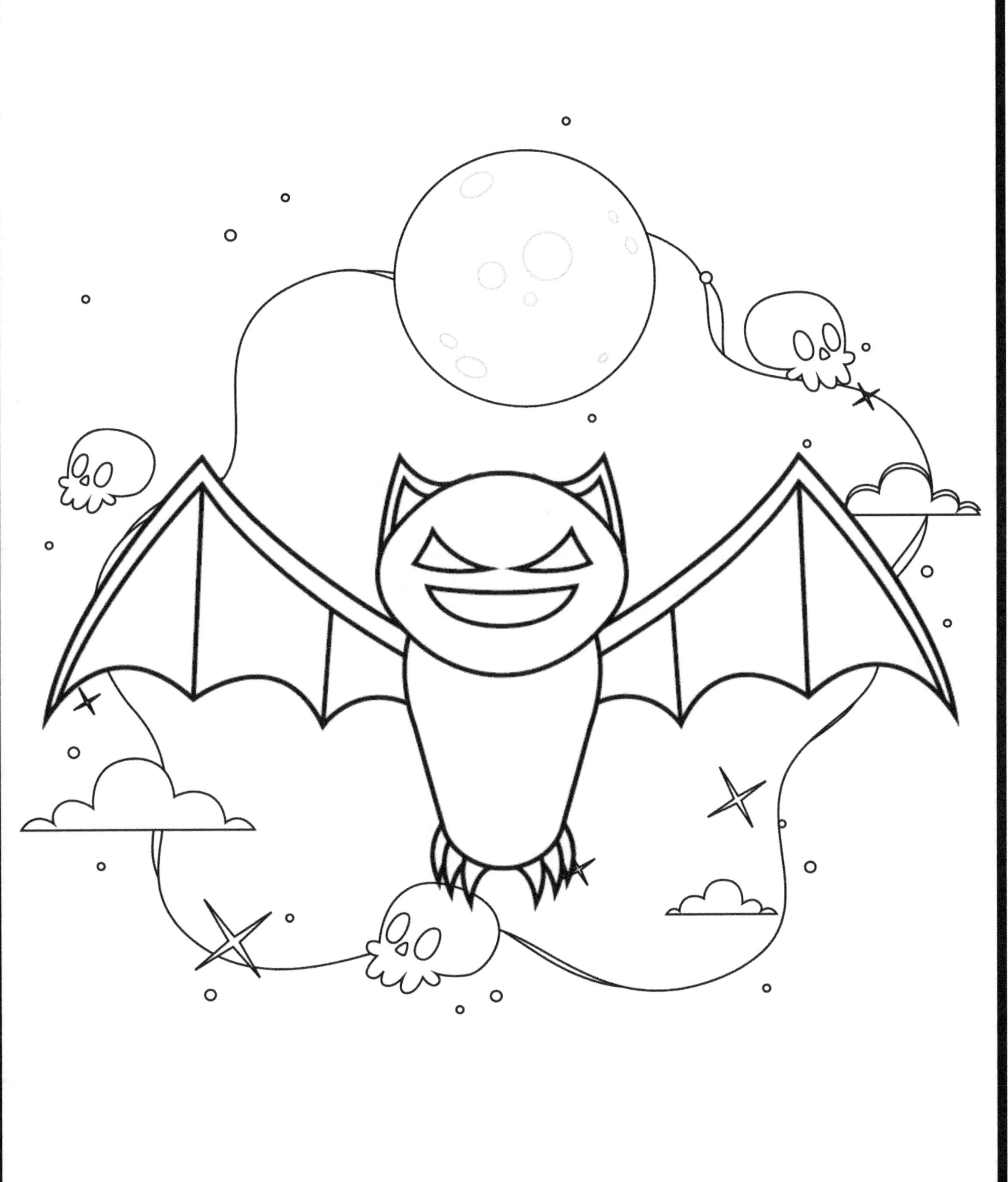

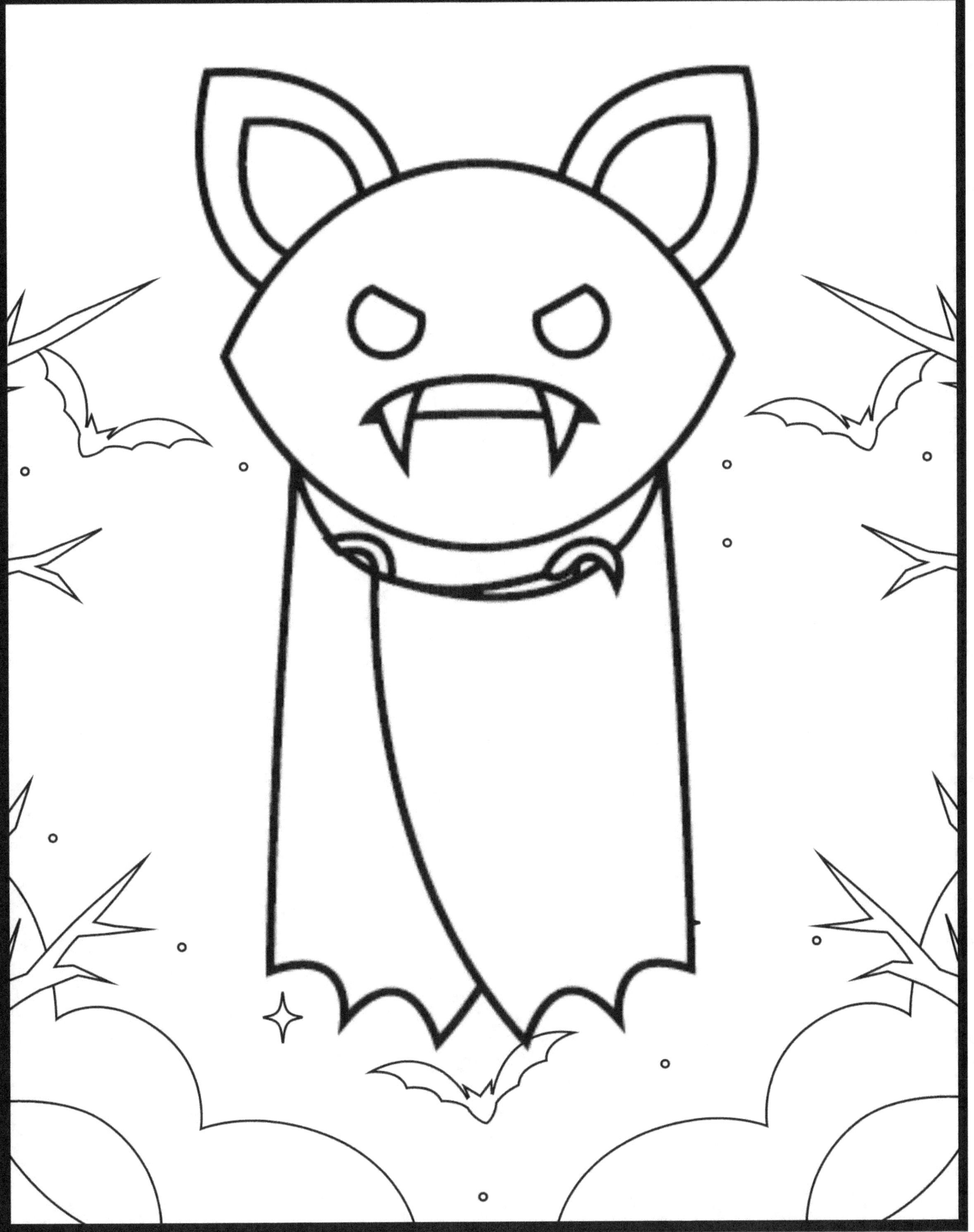

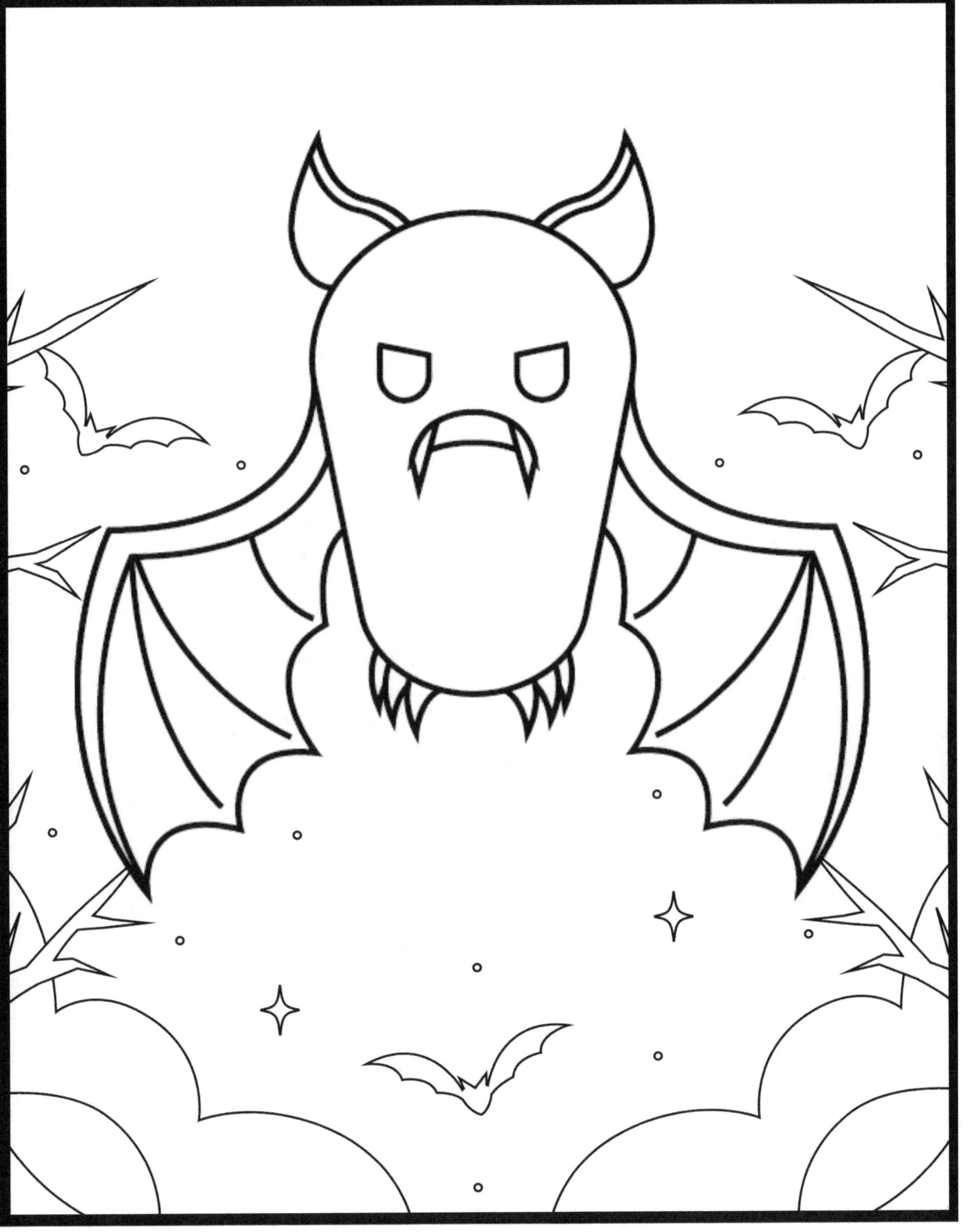

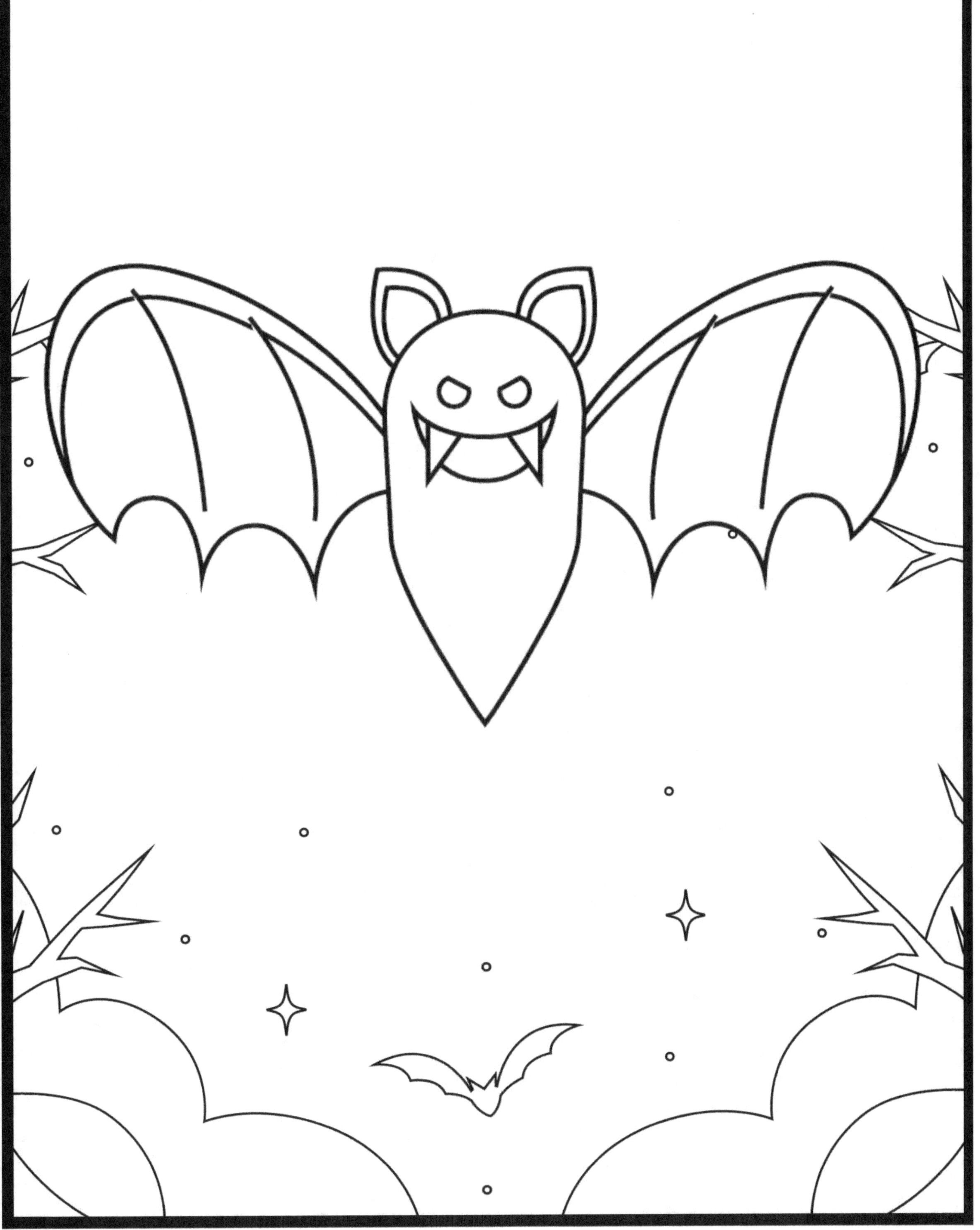

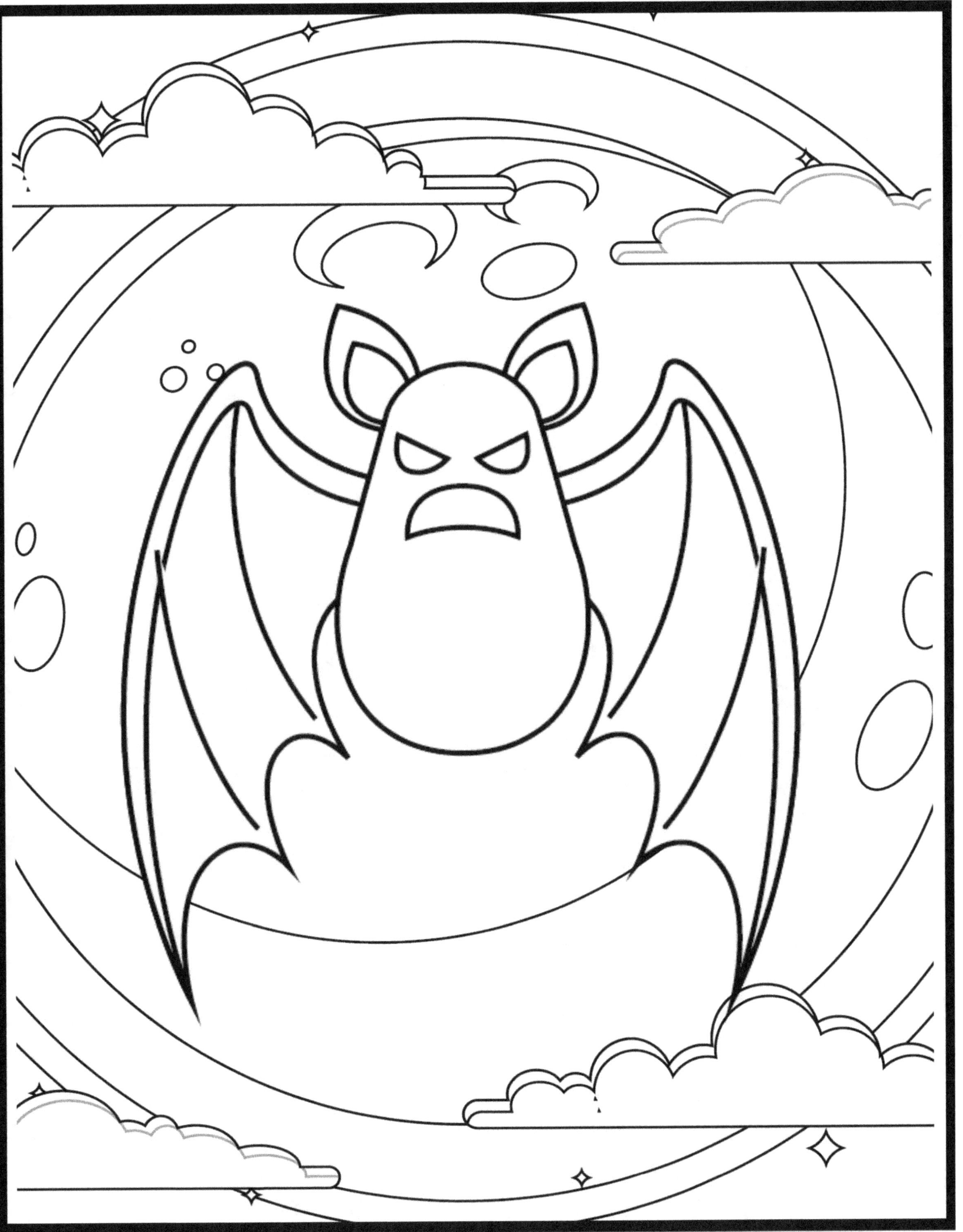